The successful strategy for business growth

I0480009

THE SUCCESSFUL

STRATEGY

FOR BUSINESS GROWTH

THE SUCCESSFUL

STRATEGY

FOR BUSINESS GROWTH

Step-by-step manual
to develop an effective strategic plan
to attract investors
and position products in new international markets

Fabrizio Nicoli, MBA

Phenomenal book, well written and lays out how to step by step prepare / develop a business strategy. A must read for anyone trying to grow their business.

Ron Guntert, CEO.
Guntert & Zimmerman Const.
San Francisco, California, USA.

It is a great guide easy to follow to do investment assessment.
It helps you put together in a comprehensive way all the MBA strategic analysis we have learned.
Thanks Fabrizio, you always find ways to improve not only your own life but also others!

Ninel Naus, Manager
Fila Surface Care solutions
Miami, Florida, USA

Many people thinks that the success of a business is given by the business idea and money to develop it. It's not enough! The business has to be developed with a strategy, with an international approach. This manual can guide you in this way, to plan, monitor, measure and have an effective strategy. Your future is important, take your time to know how to plan it

Eng. Roberto Teani, Quality Auditor.
Milan, Italy

To my Family and Friends

CONTENTS

ABOUT THIS BOOK

After reading this step-by-step manual, you will be able to:

- ✓ Understand MBA key concepts about international Strategy
- ✓ develop a professional strategic feasibility plan in order to grow your business and your brand either locally than internationally
- ✓ create the appetite Index of potential investors or the appetite Index of potential buyers-customers
- ✓ understand which information are valuable for your strategic feasibility plan, and which are not.
- ✓ understand the difference between strategy and marketing.
- ✓ master the strategic tools
- ✓ reflect on, re-evaluate and improve your performance

This book is based on my personal executive MBA mastery project carried out for the International NGO Group in renewable energy finance founded and chaired by Gov. Arnold Schwarzenegger, along with a decade of international business experience achieved in pursuing and securing business growth in international markets.

This book has achieved the Amazon number 1 bestselling position in 2019 in Italy, France, United Kingdom and 5th in USA.

I would like to thank to all the readers of *The successful strategy for business growth* that have help me to achieved the Number 1 Amazon's best-selling position in 2019 in the following Countries and categories:

Bestseller Amazon UK - United Kingdom (2019):
#1   Business and finance – Management & Leadership
#5   Small Business & Entrepreneurship
#34   MBA Business EBook

Bestseller Amazon   Italia (2019):
1   Impresa, strategia e Gestione
1   Economia, Affari e Finanza
1   ebook lingua inglese (Assoluto Italia. 30 categorie)
1   ebook lingua straniera

Bestseller Amazon France (2019):
#1   Systems & Planning
#1   Entrepreneurship

Bestseller Amazon   USA (2019)
5   Business System and planning
11   Startups

AMAZON #1 INTERNATIONAL BESTSELLER

THE SUCCESSFUL

STRATEGY

FOR BUSINESS GROWTH

MBA LEVEL
STEP-BY-STEP MANUAL
TO DEVELOP A PROFESSIONAL
INTERNATIONAL STRATEGIC PLAN

FABRIZIO NICOLI

ATTRACT INVESTMENTS AND POSITION PRODUCTS IN NEW MARKETS

Proudly became

#1 AMAZON BESTSELLER
#1 Italy, #1 UK, #1 France
#5 USA   #35 Brasil

Thank you everyone

Categories:
#1 Business & finance –
Management & Leadership (UK)
1 Impresa, strategia e Gestione
1 Economia, Affari, Finanza(ITA
#1 Systems & Planning (France)
#1 Entrepreneurship (France)
5 Business System and
planning, # 11 Startups (USA)

amazon BEST SELLER

CITY
UNIVERSITY OF LONDON
— EST 1894 —

Blogs

City Alumni Network

MBA Thesis given the 'sign' of approval by Governor Arnold Schwarzenegger

Posted on by Danielle Critchley

Alumni Stories

abrizio Nicoli (Executive MBA
Dubai 2014), shares how his
ntastic opportunity to complete
a MBA Thesis project at
overnor Arnold
chwarzenegger's not-for-profit
rganisation, R20 – Regions of
limate Change, has secured
m a representative role in the
liddle East

nd out more about Fabrizio
ere

an you tell me about your
me at Cass?

aving lived in Dubai for the last
3 years, I undertook the
xecutive MBA at the age of 31
t the institution in the United

ABOUT THE AUTHOR

Fabrizio Nicoli, Italian citizen, is a business manager, author and public speaker.

Nicoli is an MBA graduated from City University of London, CASS business school, with major in strategy and finance; holds a degree in Industrial management engineering from the University of Bergamo, Italy.

Over the past 20 years Nicoli has achieved international professional experience having been resident in Italy for 30 years, in Oxford UK, and in Dubai for more than 10 years.

His professional experiences, gained in prestigious stock exchange listed Groups, involve driving business growth, organizational change, business process optimization, corporate strategy and investment strategy.

Nicoli has appeared in leading construction magazines in the Middle East, it has been interviewed in the Italian televisions, and has spoken in more than 100 public events.

Nicoli is active in renewable energy NGO organizations.

To find out more and for any inquiries you can contact him at fabrinicoli@gmail.com or linkedin.com/in/fabrizio-nicoli-mba/

INTRODUCTION

Welcome to the *successful strategy for business growth,* a new step- by-step manual that will guide you in developing an effective strategic feasibility plan to study the Industry of your business, to design and to execute the most effective strategy with the aim to be unique among your competitive environment and to deliver the highest value to your Customers in order to exploit the local and the international market.

This book is the result of the expertise gained from the executive MBA degree of CASS Business school, City University of London, along with a decade of international business experience achieved in pursuing and reaching business growth and market internationalization.
The manual is designed for anyone that is starting a new business venture, for entrepreneurs willing to expand internationally their brand, for MBA candidates working in the

strategic sector and for anyone willing to enter in a specific market from a local to an International level.

The manual is structured to provide you an introduction to the concept of Strategy, then will guide you in understanding the strategic methods and tools to be used to analyze the Industry in which you are willing to expand, and will bring you to the final and most important part of the feasibility plan where it will be defined the Appetite Index of the Investors and of the potential customers for your business.

The approach used in describing the strategic tools, as the Porter's industry forces or the SWOT analysis, is not only a simple to-do-list or a description of the tools, but is focusing on the exact information that has to be collected from the literature and has to be analyzed in order to optimize your time and has to be followed to be able to define in a precise way the Appetite index of your customer and Investors, along with the investment criteria and viable business models to be used to succeed in your market.

The Appetite Index generated at the end of the feasibility plan will test whether private customers, institutional and public companies are willing to purchase and invest in your product and will help you to further understand which economic conditions they would be interested in order for you to expand into the selected Market.

The analysis that will be carried out is divided in two parts: a primary and a secondary research.

The primary research consists of a survey addressed to the main decision makers of your selected market, ranging from local customers to the CFOs and CEOs of the Companies that have shown an important impact in the creation of the GDP of the whole Country.

The secondary research consists in the review of the literature related to your Industry.

An in depth and critical analysis of the Industry will be carried out using strategic frameworks (Porter's five forces, PEST and SWOT analysis) and will provide unique information regarding the status of the supply and demand of your product both on a local that on a global level, information about the Industry profitability, industry competition, as well as a study of the strength and weaknesses of your brand in the view of its entrance in the target market.

During the study the main financial economic indicators of the Industry will be also analyzed and it will be described how to identify the main Industry stakeholders that are generating the highest value in the GDP of the Region.

The findings from the two researches will support you in deciding the suitable strategy to expand your brand and operations within the local or in the International market.

The final recommendations will focus on multiple strategic aspects as the value creation for the customers and the value capturing strategy, the strategy execution, the timing to enter in the market, the new value curve definition, the implementation of the Porter's differentiation strategy, the integrated marketing communications plan (IMC) and how to improve your competitive output.

At the end of the manual it is provided an extensive bibliography to direct the readers to further example and discussion.

Throughout my career the strategic MBA approach played a significant role in my success in achieving market internationalization and business growth, and I believe it can help you as well, which is why I have now created this guide on feasibility strategic planning that makes sure your business's actions will be aligned with the direction you ultimately want to go and for you to know what steps are necessary to achieve success and the most straightforward way to accomplish them.

Roadmap to write a professional Feasibility Plan

INDUSTRY DEFINITION

Which is your Industry, Who is the customer, Value preposition, levels of Strategy

SECONDARY SEARCH

Industry review, supply and demand, Porter 5 Forces, PEST, SWOT, Firm Value Chain, timing market entry, Resources and capabilities, Economic indicators

PRIMARY RESEARCH

Statistical method of research, questionnaire creation

APPETITE INDEX OF CLIENTS AND INVESTORS

Investment conditions and buying conditions.

CONCLUSIONS

Viable Strategy definition, Business models definition

CHAPTER ONE

WHAT IS STRATEGY

CHAPTER 1

WHAT IS STRATEGY

"Strategy is about setting yourself apart from the competition. It's not a matter of being better at what you do. It's a matter of being different at what you do"

Professor Michael Porter at Harvard

"However beautiful the strategy, you should occasionally look at the results"

Sir Winston Churchill

What is a strategy? Which is the difference between business strategy and corporate strategy? What is marketing and what is strategy?

These are only few of the common questions that soon or less enter in the mind of an entrepreneur, a consultant, a student, or anyone that need to develop a strategic feasibility plan.

In this chapter we will learn what is strategy, and, most important, what is not.

For instance, this guide is not a marketing book and it is not a guide to develop a business plan, but it is a step-to-step guide to support you in writing an effective strategic feasibility plan in order for you to understand the conditions under which a group of potential customers or investors or companies will be interested in buying your product, invest in your company and for you to be able to successfully enter in a new international market.

The design of the Strategic plan will then bring you in defining the business plan and the marketing plan in order to execute your new strategy. But the Strategic plan come before that.

Having clear in mind what is **not** your strategy, what is **not** your target Region and Country, what is **not** the market segment to whom you are willing to introduce your product and business, it will allow you to save time, to save manpower costs, to reduce the operational costs involved in the execution of the strategy and to reach your target earlier and with a cost efficient way, to boost the profit.

Two concepts will explain what strategy is, and how the Firms make money: by Generating Value, and by taking Value.

By **Generating Value for the Clients and the market**:
by providing something the Market wants or giving to the Market what is willing to pay on a price higher than the cost to produce it.

By **Taking Value from the market:**
by giving something unique or scarce (customers cannot buy the identical product or service from competitors or cannot buy the same service at a lower cost), and making money out of it.

According to the Industry in which is your business or in which you would like to enter, the value for the customer is certainly different. Below are shown few examples of values for the customers:

- Financial Service Industry: the value for the clients could be identified as the investment return gained in a period of time along with trustworthy of the company;
- Multiutility Industry: the customers might be looking at the service provided by the company on time along with the low cost involved in the usage of the utility and energy
- Restaurant business: the value is the quality of the food and beverage, the service provided, at a the reasonable price for each segment of Client.
- Wellness and Fitness Industry: the clients might be looking at achieving the perfect body conditions in the shorter period possible
- Construction Industry: the Client might look for a primary location for his house along with the highest quality of the

building materials used in order to fulfill the latest energy efficiency and quality standards.

The **first step in writing your strategic feasibility plan** is to define the following key points:

- **who** is the customer, and who is not:
    Which geographic Region are you willing to enter?
    which market segment are you interested in?
    which are the stakeholders, the key players, of the Industry? And who are not?
- **what** is the value proposition and what is not offered:
    Which product or service you will give to your client or Investor? what you will not give?
- **how** we deliver it and how will we not deliver it:
    How you will deliver what promised to the customer or investor, within the selected Region?

The **second step** to be studied is to define at **which level of strategy** you would like to go: Business level, Corporate or financial level.
Winning, create and capturing value in a specific business in a specific Industry, it is about *Business strategy*.
The business strategy typically involves a single business model and a single value chain, while the *Corporate Strategy* involves multiple Business models and multiple value chain activities.

From a financial point of view a good strategy maximizes the cash flow and reduces the risk of the cost of capital.

In the literature this level of strategy it included in a concept called **operational strategy** that looks at how the different functions of the business support the corporate and business strategies.

For our study we will focus on the first two levels of strategy: Business and Corporate.

Examples of the questions to be asked in order to define the level of strategy can be among the following:

Corporate strategy:
What business is the firm in?
What businesses should it be in?
How integrated should these businesses be?
These activities need to be matched to the firm's environment, its resource capabilities and the values and expectations of stakeholders.
How integrated should these businesses be?

Business strategy:
Look at how each strategic business unit (BU) try to achieve its target within its chosen area of activity.
Which products should be develop?
What approach should be taken to gain a competitive advantage?
Which markets to enter?

We talk about *Corporate strategy* when a business identifies opportunities outside its original industry, it might contemplate diversification.

When additional businesses become part of the company, the small business owner must consider corporate-level strategy.

To be effective, the company must contribute to the efficiency, profitability and competitive advantage to each business unit.

At a most basic level, corporate strategy will outline exactly what businesses you are going to engage in, and how you plan to enter and win in those markets.

It is crucially important that you have an overall corporate strategy in place, as that strategy is going to direct all of the smaller decisions that you make.

For instance, if you are running an organization that sell Cheese (F&B), you already know exactly what the corporate strategy is going to look like – you are going to sell as many kg of cheese and type of cheese as possible, at a selling price that can generate profit.

Imagine now that you run a larger organization that is going to sell cheese on a B2B level but is also going to sell equipment that are used while making cheese.

Entering into the equipment market is a completely different challenge from selling the final product themselves, so the complexity of your corporate strategy will need to rapidly increase. The Industry definition is changing (moving from the F&B to the mechanic-plant industry) along with all the stakeholders (the final clients, the distribution channels and the professionals involved in manufacturing, promoting and selling the cheese or the equipment are different)

Before you get into the strategic planning of your business, be sure you have your corporate strategy clearly defined.

When we talk about *Business strategy* we can think of this level of strategy as a 'step down' from the corporate strategy level. In other words the strategies (even more than one, according the Business units) are more specific and they usually relate to the smaller businesses within the larger organization.

Carrying over our previous example, you would do separate strategies for selling cheese and selling cheese-making equipment. You may be going after grocery stores and restaurant to sell the cheese while you may be looking at department stores to sell your equipment.

The main points to be defined now in order to proceed with a more detailed analysis are the following ones:

1. How to generate value in a specific Region
2. How to take that value from the market
3. How to make it sustainable in the long term period
4. Who, what, how, and what is not related to your strategy

THREE LEVELS OF STRATEGY

1. **Business strategy**: creating and taking value in a specific business in a specific Industry. It involves a single business model and a single value chain

2. **Corporate Strategy:** it involves multiple business models and value chain activities.

3. **Financial Strategy**: to maximize the cash flow and reduce the risk of the cost of capital. This level of strategy is included in the **operational strategy**

THE STRATEGIC FRAMEWORKS

"The essence of strategy is choosing what not to do."

Professor Michael Porter

We will now have a look to the different methodologies necessary to develop an effective strategic plan and the correct sequence to be followed in order to get useful information in the best timing and effort possible.

Even if the reader is familiar with the tools, the author recommends following the steps described in the book in order to optimize the timing, the effort, and to obtain the precise information required to calculate the appetite index of the customers and investors.

The tools are not just a detailed description of the Industry and of the stakeholders, but are tools necessary to identify the most important information within the literature and the market to plan and execute your strategy.

As previously mentioned, the results obtained by the analysis done with the tools need to be joined with the Appetite Index study that will be designed and customized on your exact needs in the last part of the manual.

Following are the methodologies that will be used in the first part of the feasibility plan:

Analysis of the external environment of the Firm:
- Industry value chain
- 5 Forces of Porter
- PEST analysis
- SWOT analysis
- Competitor analysis

Analysis of the internal environment of the Firm:
- Resources and Capabilities
- Firm Value Chain

It will be analyzed who does what in the Industry, how the profitability is shared in the Industry, how the value is created and potentially captured from the market.

STRATEGY EXECUTION: OUTCOMES

"Execution is the ability to mesh strategy with reality, align people with goals, and achieve the promised results."

Larry Bossidy
former CEO of Honeywell International Inc.

The Competitive advantage

The **third step** to be done in starting the feasibility plan is to choose how to execute the strategy and which will be the source of your competitive advantage, weather as *Cost leader* or as an *Industry differentiator.*

Bearing in mind that a unique product and business idea is mandatory in order to exploit the market, Professor Michael Porter highlight that two strategies will outperform the competitors in an industry and will establish a long term market leader position:

- **Cost leader:** to be the lower cost producer in the Industry for a fix and given level of quality.

  You aim to be the cheapest one and to exploit the economy of scale, selling more products at the lower price possible.

  Example of this strategy are the low-cost airplane companies that have been able to issue tickets to fly at prices even below 5$ per ticket.

- **Industry differentiator:** to offer a product or service at a premium price based on an unique characteristic that is valued by the customer at an higher level than the one of your competitors. The clients will be willing to pay more for the uniqueness of your product or service.

  Example of it are the premium airline companies that are offering exclusive inflight service for the customers that are willing to pay and additional mark-up for it.

A dual strategy would not be recommended in order to avoid confusion in the market about your brand and, more important, to avoid confusion in your same Organization.

Possible outcomes of the study of which competitive advantage use could be:
- to scale-up the existing business model in the new Region
- to develop a new business
- to **not** enter in the new market and to keep focusing on your existing business and brand. It might avoid a loss of money and resources.

Timing of Market Entry

The feasibility plan will bring you close to understand the correct time to enter in the selected Region and if to enter as a *Leader* or a *Follower of another market leader.*

Being a Leader, or a Market first mover, requires analyzing if:

-   You can gain access to a unique resource that will not be accessible to any of your competitors, as a new raw material or a Professional person to hire in your Company
-   You have a unique technology, and how long will take the competitors to gain a similar or even better technology
-   You can switch costs: if and when the competitor will copy what you have learned, you and your Company will need to switch product and therefore you need to take in consideration how much is going to impact the switching cost in your organization.

The Market leader often get the first-mover advantage in new markets. Let's look at some examples of market leaders in the digital space. Microsoft was the first company to launch the operating system (Windows) and web browser (Internet Explorer) in the market. Apple as a company was the first one to introduce the concept of portable media device in which music can be stored on a drive, iPod.

Market leadership is not about sales and dominance but it is more about how relevant the product is for the audience. Apple generates more revenue by selling iPods compared to other manufacturers who are selling MP3 players. It is all about innovative ideas which will help the company to connect with the relevant audience.

The company may also attract the customers of competitors by figuring out the ideal combination of quality and price. In this modern age of the internet, it is easy to identify consumer-oriented market leaders - Apple, Google, Amazon, and Facebook all qualify. In capital goods, Boeing and Caterpillar are other two examples.

At the other side **the market followers** is a Company that might not even try to challenge the leader, and is only trying to keep its market share.
There are some pro in being a followers, as the opportunity to look at the mistake of the leader and gain experience and market share out of it, or the fact to have less R&D costs and more operational flexibility
Followers might also become leaders, as Google has done entering in the market after Altavista and Yahoo.

TEN THINGS

You should know about Strategy Pitfalls

1. Confusing the Strategy with Vision and Mission and with the Data Analysis
2. Not Giving importance to Resource Allocation, that is the link between Strategy Formulation and Execution
3. Failing to align Strategy with the Organization Culture and Capabilities. The Culture must be changed or alligned with the Strategy
4. Not having good measures and feedback system
5. Failing to make choices in the Value generation and Value collection
6. Failing to identify the unique strategic position
7. Confusing Strategy with short terms goals. The company has to be profitable and sustainable for the long term
8. Believing that only Top executive can have good strategic ideas
9. Having a secret strategy, hidden to the suppliers, customers and employees. We need to comunicate it to be credible
10. Believing that the competitive advantage is forever. The drivers of competitive advantage has to be renewed

CHAPTER TWO

METHODOLOGY
&
KEY STRATEGIC INDICATORS

CHAPTER 2

METHODOLOGY

"The worst strategic mistake that companies make is failure to make difficult choices."

Michael Porter

The aim of this chapter is to test whether the investors (composed of private investors, institutional investors and public companies) are willing to invest in your Company or the potential Clients of your selected Region are willing to buy your Product and to find under which economic conditions they would be interested in doing it.

The analysis will be done in two parts: primary and secondary research.

The findings from the primary and secondary research will support the conclusions and the recommendations to exploit and succeed in the selected Region.

THE PRIMARY AND SECONDARY RESEARCHES

The **primary research** is a survey designed to investigate and analyze the *appetite* of the potential Clients and potential investors towards your product: the Primary research is specific to your company's needs. Rather than scouring through general information, this research is specifically tailored to you, where you can establish exact information about the marketing of your product in the chosen market.

To do so we first need to identify the so called *statistical reference market*, which includes the industrial and services sector impacting the most on the wealth creation and GDP growth in your selected Region, along with the *selected statistical sample within the reference market,* that will be based on authoritative business sources as Forbes magazine list of companies or chamber of commerce lists.
The guidelines to carry out the Primary search and to identify the above mentioned markets and sample will be described in the Chapter 4, after the secondary search.

Despite the name "primary and secondary", the correct sequence to be done in developing the study and the feasibility plan is to invert them, therefore to carry out the first the "secondary search' and then the "primary search". The reason behind it is that the strategic tools applied during the secondary search will support you in designing the primary search in the most effective way.

The **secondary research** will analyze the global and local supply of your product or service, the demand of it, the social, political, economic and competitive landscaping that you will face in the selected Region.

To carry out a secondary research it is required to analyze reports and **international economic sources** as:
- Academic and University literature
- Ministry of Economy reports
- IMF- International monetary fund - reports
- Bloomberg Finance
- World Bank
- Industry magazine and newspaper;
- Interviews with renowned experts in your Industry.
- Chamber of Commerce, Department for International Trade and the Institute of Export
- United Nations Commodity Trade Database

Research is also about understanding and responding to consumer tastes in your target market, which may be very different to your customers back home

The secondary research will face few challenges:
- **Unavailable data:** in many developing countries data are often unavailable. I suggestion to overcome this challenge is to double check the data shown by the statistic departments of the governments, and the data shown online by important sources as IMF and World Bank.
- **Out of date data:** Online can be seen reports for different countries done by different companies which look very similar as they are based on the same document but have been adapted for each country and can be out of date by the time they are published.

- **Reliability of the data:** before using quantitative data it is important to know about the data collection methodology, the purpose of the collection of the data, the consistency of the data collection and the company responsible for collecting the data.
- **Industry definition**: industry and product data classifications need to be clearly understood as some country or research companies have broader definitions which then make the data unusable.

These challenges, if ignored, can damage the credibility of your market research, leaving you unable to act on the results.
To overcome the uncertainty of the data, the primary research will support you in tailoring a new data search and to generate your correct market appetite index

> **REMEMBER**
>
> The secondary research is shown before the primary search to detail the study of the Industry from a Global scale to the finer details within the Selected Region

The secondary research will be shown before the primary search in order to detail the study of the Industry from a Global scale to the finer details within Selected Region. Following this, the primary research will provide greater detail of the industry analyzing the profile and the appetite of the prospect clients within the selected Region.

The industry will be analyzed using strategic frameworks that will highlight unique information regarding the five Forces of Porter impacting on the industry profitability, the political economical technologic and social analysis of the Industry (PEST) as well as a study of the strength, weaknesses, threats and opportunities (SWOT).

WHAT TO CONSIDER

When researching a market

1. Customers' needs for the product or the service
2. Buyer behavior and decision making process
3. Distribution channels, players and policies
4. Competitors
5. Existing customer and their opinion

INDUSTRY DEFINITION

"We don't like their sound, and guitar music is on the way out"

Decca Recording Co. rejecting the Beatles 1962

The starting point of the analysis is to define the Industry in which your products and brand belong or are going to be set.
This will impact on the study of the Industry along with your competitors and your Clients and Investors' appetite.
The better you know and understand the industry the better you will be able to determine elements that will make you stand out, be unique and reach a higher average return than the industry average.
For instance the global media and entertainment (M&E) Industry is wider than the Video Games Industry, that is included in it along with the television Industry, streaming industry, music and audio recordings Industry.

It is important to understand **what is not** your Industry in order to narrow the areas of the analysis: as example the manufacturing Industry includes the automotive industry, that includes companies and organizations involved in the design, development, manufacturing, marketing and selling of motor vehicle, but it doesn't include industries dedicated to the maintenance of automobiles such as automobile repair shops and motor fuel filling stations.

Whether you are setting up a new company or a new brand, or you have a well-established company, in order to introduce you to your prospect Clients or Investor and help them to recognize you, always include in the feasibility plan a clear statement of:

- your Mission and Vision
- business references to prove your commitment and success and to boost your credibility among the stakeholders
- management structure of the company, that is considered one of the deciding factors reviewed when deciding whether or not to invest in the Organization
- **Value proposition**, that defines your key competitive advantages and how you will delivery your uniqueness to the clients and to the industry's stakeholders:
  1. What do you offer to your Clients?
  2. How your Clients will get a positive ROI return of investment?
  3. Who are your clients? Who are not your clients?
  4. How you will deliver the value proposition to them?
  5. Which is your uniqueness?

MAJOR INDUSTRIES

In which your business should be

1. Aerospace industry
2. Agriculture (Fishing industry; Tobacco industry)
3. Chemical industry (Pharmaceutical industry)
4. Computer industry
5. Construction industry
6. Defense industry
7. Education industry
8. Energy industry (Electrical power industry, petroleum)
9. Entertainment industry
10. Financial services industry (Insurance industry)
11. Food industry
12. Health care industry
13. Hospitality industry
14. Information industry
15. Manufacturing (Automotive, electronics industry)
16. Mass media (TV, Film industry, music, news, publishing)
17. Mining
18. Telecommunications industry (Internet)
19. Transport industry
20. Service

We are now going to describe how to carry out the analysis of the Supply and the Demand of your product within the selected Region.

The **supply** can be divided into two distinct elements:

- Growing capacity supplied by each technology or each Company having the same business in the Region
- Growing number of new similar products and their expected grow in the future.

You should take these trends into consideration because the clients will require a higher value, and the investor a higher return of investment, in order to be motivated in choosing your product as the numbers of companies competing for the same market segmentation have increased.

To describe the trend of the **demand** for your product the analysis will have to be focused on two additional points:

- Flow of investments and flow of products that on a global scale are going into your industry, evidence that the prospect clients are looking for your products and their *buying or investment appetite* is high;
- Definition of the appetite index and the demand type to be found out with the primary research (see Chapter 4).

Demand indicators to be studied are among the followings:

- **population growth rate**: the growth in the number of the population might have a consequent growing demand for all the products (see table in the next page), having a good level of wealth conditions and socio political economic stability.
- **foreign investments flow**: if they are increasing rapidly from established markets such as Europe, the US and China towards new emerging markets, there will be growing demands of products (see table in the next pages to analyze the flow of investments).
- **bank system**: when the bank system appears healthy is potentially having capital to be invested into products and projects
- **venture capitalist /private equity** new investment analysis
- **distribution** of the national **population** by:
  - urban, intermediate and rural regions;
  - gender and age
- **International imports and exports** in goods and services. The value of the import of products in a Region or a Country will provide you an important indicator of the potentiality of its market.
- **health rate** (Life expectancy, Smoking rate, Overweight, Health expenditure)
- **household income and wealth rate**: National income per capita, Household disposable income, poverty rates and gaps
- **Globalization rate**: International merchandise trade, International trade in services, Foreign direct investment flows, FDI regulatory restrictiveness index, Balance of payments.

TO READ MORE

The indicators previously described related to the **Supply** and **Demands** of products and Investments, divided by industry and Region, can be found in these important professional websites:

1. IMF international monetary fund
World Economic Outlook databases and the Global Financial Stability Report.
www.imf.org/en/Data

2. United Nations Data
https://unstats.un.org/unsd/databases.htm
It provides a free access to detailed **global trade Data** and **Industrial commodity production**.
It is a collection of official international trade statistics and relevant analytical tables, including statistics of overall industrial growth, detailed data on business structure and statistics on major indicators of industrial performance by Country.

3. UN DATA United Nations Statistics Division
http://data.un.org/Browse.aspx?d=ICS
It provides a variety of statistical resources compiled by the United Nations (UN) statistical system and other international agencies, as the Food and Agriculture Organization, International Telecommunication Organization, The World Bank, UNESCO institute for Statistic, United Nations Development program, UN for the Climate change, World Health Organization, World Meteorological Organization, World Tourism Organization.

4. Countries Factbook

www.oecd-ilibrary.org/economics/oecd-factbook_18147364

It provides data, excel tables and statistics related to population and migration; production; household income, wealth and debt; globalization, trade and foreign direct investment (FDI); prices, interest rates and exchange rates; energy and transportation; labor, employment and unemployment; science and technology including research and development (R&D); environment including natural resources, water, air and climate; education resources and outcomes; government expenditures, debt, revenues, taxes, foreign aid; health status, risk and resources.

5. Export information by Industry

www.export.gov/industries

It provides latest market intelligence, trade events, trade leads.

It is provided an example of data in the next pages.

6. Countries commercial guides

www.export.gov/ccg

It provides Market conditions, opportunities, regulations, and business customs for over 125 Countries

It is a valuable source in order to get the full updated list of the requirements in terms of:

Doing business in the Country, Market challenges, Market opportunities, Market entry strategy, political and economic environment, selling products and services, leading sectors for exports and investments, customs, regulations, trade barriers, Web resources, import tariffs, import requirements and documentation, labeling/marking requirements, prohibited and restricted imports, customs regulations, standards for trade, trade agreements, licensing requirements for professional services, investment climate statement, trade and project financing, business travel.

7. Bloomberg finance
www.bloomberg.com
Global leader in business and financial data, news and insight

8. World Investments projection
www.iea.org/weo/

9. Standard & Poor's Rating Services
www.standardandpoors.com

10. Moody's analytics risk management
www.moodysanalytics.com

11. World Bank group indicators
International Development, Poverty, Sustainability. Global trends and future prospects   www.worldbank.org/en/research

12. Financial trend forecast   https://fintrend.com/

13. Market Assessment report, by Industry
Reports done by the International trade administration
www.trade.gov/topmarkets/
It provides Markets Reports for the main Industries:
Agricultural Equipment, Aircraft Parts, Automotive Parts, Building Products & Sustainable Construction, Civil Nuclear, Cloud Computing, Construction Equipment, Education, Environmental Tech, Franchising, Industrial Automation, Manufacturing Technology, Media & Entertainment, Medical

Devices, Oil & Gas Equipment, Pharmaceuticals, Renewable Energy, Travel and Tourism

14. OECD
(Organisation for Economic Cooperation & Development)
Countries reports
www.oecd-ilibrary.org/
It provides reports, statistics, projections and other information on a number of socio-economic themes as: Agriculture & Food, Education, Employment, Energy, Environment, Finance and Investment, Governance, Industry and Services, Social Issues / Migration / Health, Taxation, Trade, Transport, Urban, Rural and Regional Development

Practical example of the Demand indicators are shown in the next pages, along with the website where they can be found for your further analysis and to customize the study and research on your selected Country

Example of Import - Export information by Industry
Imports of Paints,coatings and adhesives

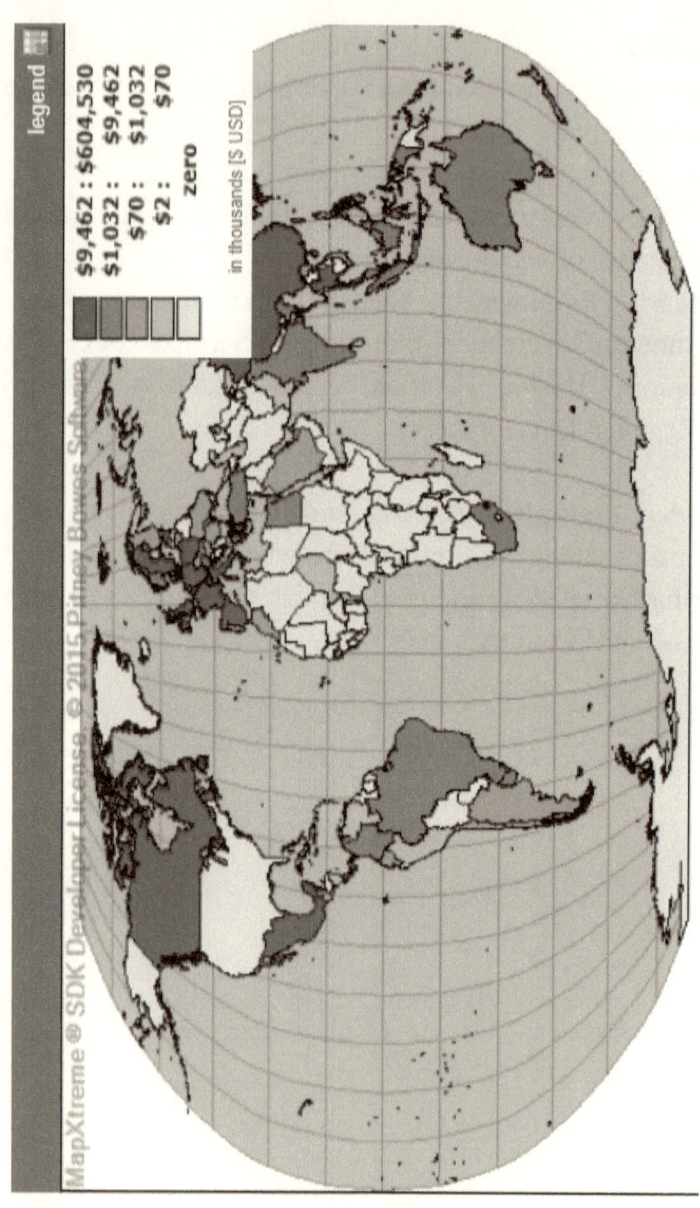

legend

$9,462 : $604,530
$1,032 : $9,462
   $70 : $1,032
    $2 : $70
       zero

in thousands [$ USD]

MapXtreme ® SDK Developer License © 2015 Pitney Bowes Software

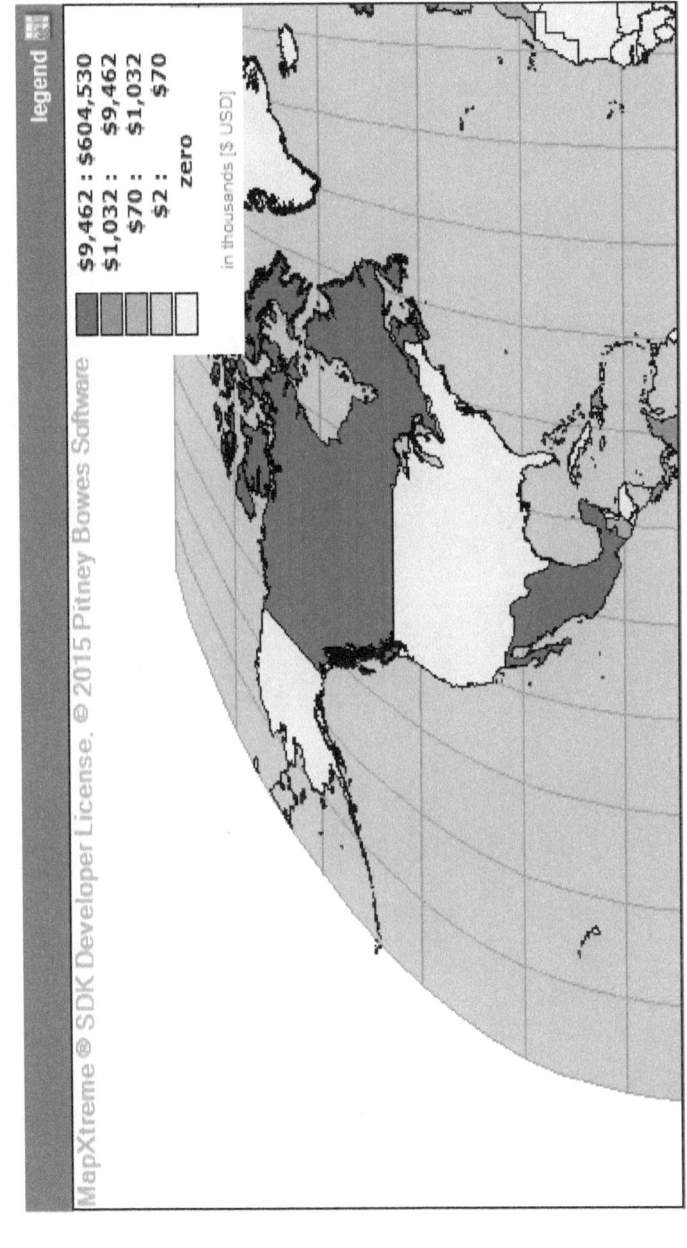

2018 Imports of NAICS 3255--PAINTS, COATINGS & ADHESIVES

Imports of NAICS 3255—PAINTS, COATINGS & ADHESIVES

Partner	2014	2015	2016	2017	2018 ▽
World	1,682,853,656	1,676,490,671	1,762,490,345	1,937,898,480	2,102,163,119
Canada	474,393,132	499,418,915	531,841,018	547,233,371	604,529,729
Germany	302,733,813	276,608,826	271,429,886	305,937,982	336,891,626
China	124,944,081	133,198,295	131,273,879	177,771,517	184,728,715
Japan	126,960,053	136,956,317	138,773,527	150,959,190	160,373,889
Mexico	151,295,252	124,383,568	137,483,692	147,423,619	151,409,749
South Korea	49,602,797	66,737,980	72,605,476	89,099,767	92,865,612
United Kingdom	62,983,831	80,487,266	65,615,554	88,215,641	72,573,016
France	46,852,359	45,823,262	48,811,141	58,833,415	65,038,237
Italy	52,199,407	45,691,073	48,443,003	51,955,616	64,831,284
Netherlands	44,271,982	44,998,330	55,334,616	57,135,699	61,158,103
Belgium	28,407,023	28,808,679	31,827,582	35,941,315	40,353,858
Sweden	26,615,173	27,299,482	30,882,888	32,554,004	34,183,682
Taiwan	20,000,277	20,173,836	25,271,786	26,119,719	28,072,671
Liechtenstein	2,018,127	10,991,427	10,034,258	18,082,504	28,006,447
Spain	20,083,280	20,260,375	20,390,120	20,274,973	23,980,558
Ireland	17,700,581	16,277,381	26,704,411	27,022,529	22,111,643
Switzerland	18,208,708	23,781,817	18,969,538	18,900,498	20,913,696
Poland	7,769,548	8,942,239	10,532,170	13,743,745	14,179,401
Estonia	5,203,580	4,178,571	7,750,032	6,271,231	12,853,530
Thailand	5,091,102	5,715,481	5,730,785	7,527,201	9,462,638
Turkey	8,164,467	8,099,483	6,735,604	7,860,746	8,356,084
Australia	6,189,453	7,300,293	8,136,145	8,217,496	8,031,640
Colombia	3,423,192	3,307,740	3,709,149	3,328,106	6,598,728

Source: Foreign Trade Division, U.S. Census Bureau.
www.export.gov/industries
http://tse.export.gov/tse/MapDisplay.aspx

Example of Import - Export information by Industry
Exports of Alcoholic Beverages

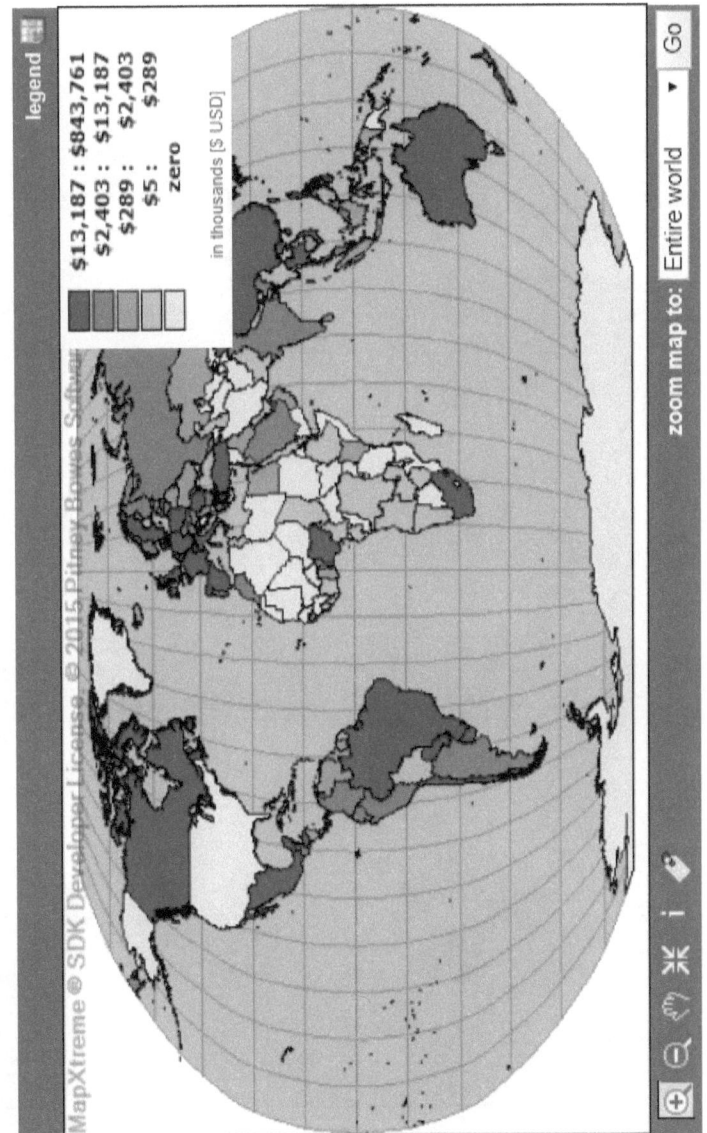

2018 Exports of SITC 112--Alcoholic Beverages

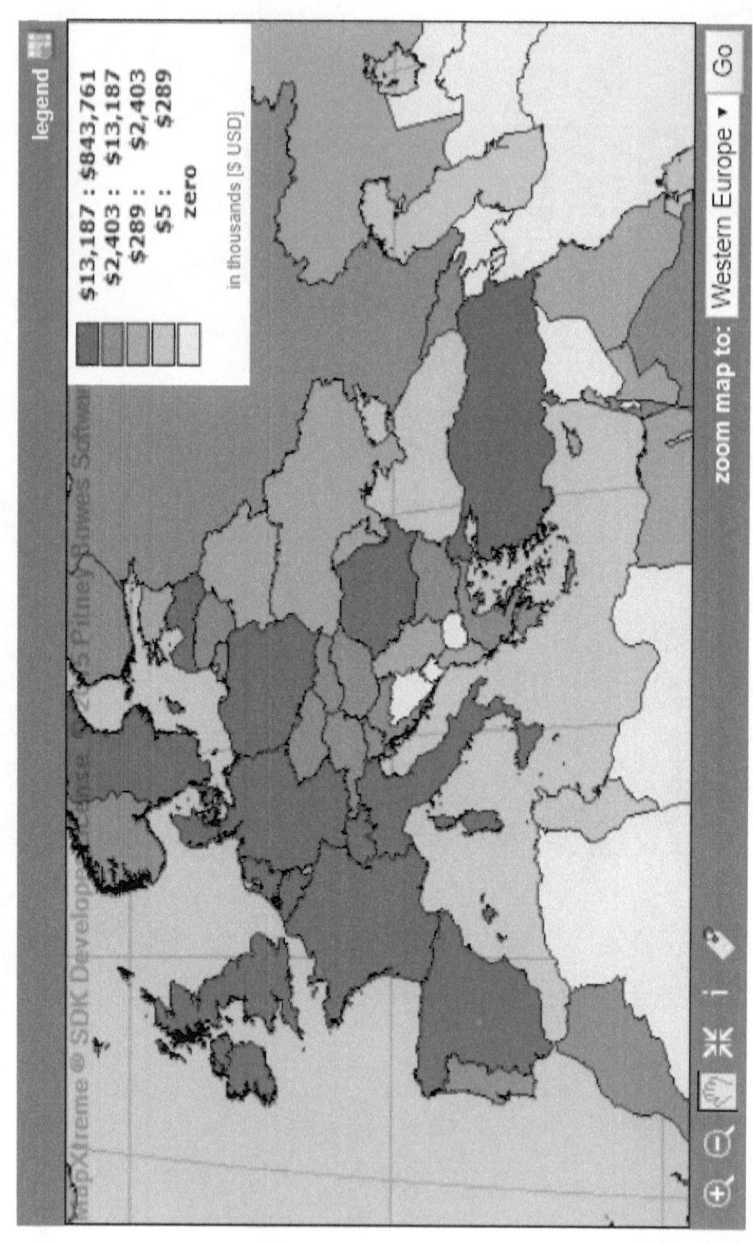

Exports of SITC 112—Alcoholic Beverages

Partner	2014	2015	2016	2017	2018 ▽
World	4,074,887,023	4,231,808,461	4,135,740,800	4,357,914,749	4,487,669,635
Canada	916,222,364	858,004,067	826,885,290	859,415,620	843,760,678
United Kingdom	420,489,988	539,879,990	490,783,697	460,053,197	459,394,038
Panama	149,606,116	218,620,587	235,657,812	254,793,216	263,290,947
Mexico	304,527,385	276,380,085	242,140,552	232,607,701	253,782,248
Japan	195,200,395	215,580,198	194,572,543	217,749,161	217,069,190
Netherlands	177,836,305	181,878,479	205,320,115	203,692,220	201,145,099
France	151,225,275	132,180,925	160,661,452	180,994,908	199,536,139
Hong Kong	106,698,146	119,672,667	123,230,503	152,542,654	173,368,345
Germany	202,981,921	223,525,134	194,105,239	224,103,249	170,745,839
Australia	160,322,893	152,024,738	137,132,364	149,461,946	138,101,810
Viet Nam	36,833,176	37,801,747	73,759,934	51,157,160	123,706,595
Spain	84,682,651	88,922,037	106,274,303	126,828,821	123,672,443
Chile	61,361,360	63,392,662	72,789,627	112,994,518	100,853,797
China	95,380,854	78,842,694	102,949,169	100,034,123	87,242,057
South Korea	42,473,500	43,028,371	41,592,183	61,307,714	76,019,959
Singapore	68,984,618	56,308,953	56,251,603	62,152,534	70,111,712
Italy	84,861,058	68,913,477	63,212,367	48,665,863	57,674,248
Denmark	35,585,867	35,793,560	33,808,218	39,714,855	56,901,610
Belgium	49,688,443	45,326,415	56,527,181	60,307,708	49,868,378
Latvia	28,124,442	46,212,820	31,135,997	42,416,164	49,190,062
Sweden	47,664,898	59,359,958	52,223,645	50,031,585	45,037,249
Poland	41,829,945	59,286,797	54,273,205	38,275,243	43,112,325
Brazil	18,102,318	24,953,326	14,584,033	36,343,665	39,580,809
Dominican Republic	24,518,845	30,407,526	29,112,828	29,337,952	35,594,185

Source: Foreign Trade Division, U.S. Census Bureau.
http://tse.export.gov/tse/MapDisplay.aspx

Example of Commodity trade statistic available from the UN DATA organization, United Nations Statistics Division
The Trade of **JAPAN** related to **Dairy products**.

Country: JAPAN - Year 2017 - Import Export			
Commodity	Flow	Trade (USD)	Weight (kg)
Milk not concentrated nor sweetened < 1% fat	Export	180,635	103,248
Milk not concentrated nor sweetened 1-6% fat	Import	47,321	51,396
Milk not concentrated nor sweetened 1-6% fat	Export	8,873,421	4,622,487
Milk powder < 1.5% fat	Import	130,823,418	58,541,599
Milk powder < 1.5% fat	Export	347,226	33,343
Yogurt	Import	70,264	22,584
Yogurt	Export	536,413	105,620
Buttermilk, curdled milk, cream, kephir, etc.	Import	72,680	6,151
Buttermilk, curdled milk, cream, kephir, etc.	Export	318,194	62,541
Whey	Import	97,698,916	57,021,040
Whey	Export	7,017	400
Natural milk products nes	Import	35,361,460	9,799,432
Natural milk products nes	Export	3,522,866	786,283
Butter and other fats and oils derived from milk	Import	47,453,134	8,167,503
Butter and other fats and oils derived from milk	Export	71,584	4,028
Fresh cheese, unfermented whey cheese, curd	Import	387,403,982	94,104,079
Fresh cheese, unfermented whey cheese, curd	Export	1,111,979	87,949
Cheese, grated or powdered, of all kinds	Import	47,129,403	4,953,045
Cheese, grated or powdered, of all kinds	Export	23,139	1,020
Cheese processed, not grated or powdered	Import	36,526,065	7,309,866
Cheese processed, not grated or powdered	Export	5,867,440	517,399
Cheese, blue-veined	Import	11,931,521	1,082,606
Cheese except fresh, grated, processed or blue-veined	Import	679,306,523	165,321,953
Cheese except fresh, grated, processed or blue-veined	Export	2,369,603	143,462
Birds eggs, in shell, fresh, preserved or cooked	Import	5,847,199	1,903,417
Birds eggs, in shell, fresh, preserved or cooked	Export	9,557,335	3,933,628
Egg yolks dried	Import	11,820,740	2,589,591
Egg yolks dried	Export	11,690	120
Eggs, bird, not in shell, dried	Import	9,642,944	2,419,625
Eggs, bird, not in shell, dried	Export	1,173,959	31,910
Honey, natural	Import	143,010,858	42,820,623
Honey, natural	Export	272,576	20,798

Source: Commodity Trade Statistics Database | United Nations Statistics Division   http://data.un.org/Browse.aspx?d=ICS

Example of Service- Tourism Industry -Expenditures

The same detail, by Country, can be obtained also for services.
In the below example is shown the flow of inbond and outbond
Turist visiting or exiting Australia, along with their expenditure

AUSTRALIA	2010	2011	2012	2013	2014	2015	2016	2017
Inbound tourism								
Arrivals - Thousands	5 790	5 771	6 032	6 482	6 922	7 450	8 269	8 815
Tourism expenditure in the country - US$ Mn	31 064	34 315	34 137	32 889	33 619	30 872	36 786	43 982
Travel - US$ Mn	28 472	31 582	31 557	30 617	31 452	28 892	34 746	41 754
Passenger transport - US$ Mn	2 592	2 733	2 580	2 272	2 167	1 980	2 040	2 228
Outbound tourism								
Departures - Thousands	7 103	7 788	8 212	9 052	9 480	9 807	10 380	10 932
Tourism expenditure in other countries - US$ Mn	27 851	33 967	35 226	35 197	32 462	28 614	32 923	39 491
Travel - US$ Mn	22 558	27 371	28 078	28 575	26 919	23 734	28 044	34 251
Passenger transport - US$ Mn	5 293	6 596	7 148	6 622	5 543	4 880	4 879	5 240

INBOUND TOURISM: Arrivals of non resident tourists/visitors - thousands
INBOUND TOURISM: Tourism expenditure in the country (credit) - US$ million
OUTBOUND TOURISM: Departures - trips abroad by resident tourists/visitors - thousands
OUTBOUND TOURISM: Tourism expenditure in other countries (debit) - US$ million

Source: World Tourism Data | World Tourism Organization
http://data.un.org/DocumentData.aspx?id=401

It is provided below the table showing the **population growth (or decrease)** of the main Countries (in thousands).

	2007	2008	2009	2010	2011	2012	2013
Australia	20 828	21 249	21 692	22 032	22 340	22 728	23 126
Austria	8 295	8 322	8 341	8 361	8 389	8 426	8 469
Belgium	10 626	10 710	10 796	10 920	11 048	11 128	11 178
Canada	32 928	33 318	33 727	34 127	34 484	34 880	35 154
Chile	16 505	16 687	16 877	17 066	17 256	17 445	17 632
Czech Republic	10 323	10 430	10 491	10 517	10 497	10 509	10 511
Denmark	5 461	5 494	5 523	5 548	5 571	5 592	5 615
Estonia	1 341	1 337	1 335	1 331	1 327	1 323	1 318
Finland	5 289	5 313	5 339	5 363	5 388	5 414	5 439
France	61 965	62 300	62 615	62 918	63 223	63 514	63 786
Germany	82 257	82 135	81 904	81 715	80 249	80 413	80 611
Greece	11 163	11 186	11 185	11 153	11 124	11 090	..
Hungary	10 056	10 038	10 023	10 000	9 972	9 920	9 893
Iceland	311	319	319	318	319	321	324
Ireland	4 376	4 485	4 533	4 555	4 575	4 585	4 593
Italy	58 272	58 740	59 140	59 420	59 660	59 898	60 225
Japan	127 771	127 692	127 510	128 057	127 799	127 515	127 298
Korea	48 598	48 949	49 182	49 410	49 779	50 004	50 220
Luxembourg	476	484	494	502	512	525	537
Mexico	109 787	111 299	112 853	114 256	115 683	117 054	118 395
Netherlands	16 382	16 446	16 530	16 615	16 693	16 755	16 804
New Zealand	4 224	4 260	4 303	4 351	4 384	4 408	4 442
Norway	4 709	4 768	4 829	4 889	4 953	5 019	5 080
Poland	38 116	38 116	38 153	38 517	38 526	38 534	38 502
Portugal	10 543	10 558	10 568	10 573	10 558	10 515	10 457
Slovak Republic	5 375	5 379	5 386	5 391	5 398	5 408	5 416
Slovenia	2 019	2 023	2 042	2 049	2 052	2 056	2 059
Spain	45 236	45 983	46 368	46 562	46 736	46 766	46 593
Sweden	9 148	9 220	9 299	9 378	9 449	9 519	9 609
Switzerland	7 551	7 648	7 744	7 828	7 912	7 997	8 140
Turkey	70 158	71 052	72 039	73 142	74 224	75 176	76 055
United Kingdom	60 482	60 982	61 424	61 915	62 435	62 859	63 238
United States	301 231	304 094	306 772	309 347	311 722	314 112	316 498
Brazil	189 954	192 000	193 995	193 253	197 825	199 689	201 467
China	1 334 344	1 342 733	1 351 248	1 359 822	1 368 440	1 377 065	1 385 567
India	1 159 095	1 174 662	1 190 138	1 205 625	1 221 156	1 236 687	1 252 140
Indonesia	230 973	234 244	237 487	240 677	243 802	246 864	249 866
Russian Federation	142 805	142 742	142 785	142 849	142 961	143 207	143 507
South Africa	48 658	49 345	50 055	50 792	51 554	52 341	53 158

The successful strategy for business growth

It is provided below the table showing the population growth by sex and age.
Additional details for your studies can be found at this link:
unstats.un.org/unsd/demographic-social/products/dyb/dyb_2017/

Population by sex, annual rate of population increase, surface area and density								
Continent, country or area and census date	Population at the latest available census (in units)			Mid-year estimates (in thousands)		Annual rate of increase	Surface area (km²)	Density
	Both sexes	Male	Female	2010	2017	2010-17	2017	2017
EUROPE								
Albania - Albanie	2,800,138	1,403,059	1,397,079	2,913	2,873	...	28,748	100
Austria - Autriche	8,401,940	4,093,938	4,308,002	8,361	8,773	0.7	83,882	105
Belarus - Bélarus	9,503,807	4,420,039	5,083,768	9,491	9,498	0.0	207,600	46
Belgium - Belgique	11,000,638	5,401,718	5,598,920	10,896	11,382	0.6	30,528	373
Bosnia and Herzegovina - Bosnie-Herzégovine	3,531,159	1,732,270	1,798,889	3,843	3,510	...	51,209	69
Bulgaria - Bulgarie	7,364,570	3,586,571	3,777,999	7,534	7,076	-0.9	110,372	64
Croatia - Croatie	4,284,889	2,066,335	2,218,554	4,295	4,130	-0.6	56,594	73
Czechia - Tchéquie	10,436,560	5,109,766	5,326,794	10,474	10,594	0.2	78,870	134
Denmark - Danemark	5,560,628	2,756,582	2,804,046	5,545	5,761	0.5	42,921	134
Estonia - Estonie	1,294,455	600,526	693,929	1,331	1,317	-0.2	45,227	29
Finland - Finlande	5,375,276	2,638,416	2,736,860	5,335	5,508	0.5	336,866	16
France	61,399,541	29,714,539	31,685,002	62,918	64,910	0.4	551,500	118
Germany - Allemagne	80,219,695	39,145,941	41,073,754	81,757	82,522	0.1	357,578	231
Greece - Grèce	10,816,286	5,303,223	5,513,063	11,121	10,768	-0.5	131,957	82
Hungary - Hongrie	9,937,628	4,718,479	5,219,149	10,000	9,788	-0.3	93,022	105
Ireland - Irlande	4,761,865	2,354,428	2,407,437	4,560	4,784	0.7	69,825	69
Italy - Italie	59,433,744	28,745,507	30,688,237	59,277	60,537	0.3	302,073	200
Latvia - Lettonie	2,070,371	946,102	1,124,269	2,098	1,942	-1.1	64,573	30
Lithuania - Lituanie	3,043,429	1,402,604	1,640,825	3,097	2,828	-1.3	65,286	43
Luxembourg	512,353	254,967	257,386	507	596	2.3	2,586	231
Malta - Malte	417,432	207,625	209,807	415	468	1.7	315	1,486
Montenegro - Monténégro	620,029	306,236	313,793	619	622	0.1	13,812	45
Netherlands - Pays-Bas	16,655,799	8,243,482	8,412,317	16,615	17,100	0.4	41,543	412
Norway - Norvège	4,979,955	2,495,777	2,484,178	4,889	5,277	1.1	323,772	16
Poland - Pologne	38,044,565	18,420,389	19,624,176	38,042	37,975	0.0	312,679	121
Portugal	10,282,306	4,868,755	5,413,551	10,573	10,300	-0.4	92,226	112
Romania - Roumanie	20,039,141	9,736,342	10,302,799	20,247	19,644	...	238,391	82
Russian Federation - Fédération de Russie	143,436,145	66,457,074	76,979,071	142,849		...	17,098,246	...
Serbia - Serbie	7,186,862	3,499,176	3,687,686	7,291	7,021	-0.5	88,417	79
Slovakia - Slovaquie	5,397,036	2,627,772	2,769,264	5,391	5,439	0.1	49,035	111
Slovenia - Slovénie	2,062,874	1,022,229	1,040,645	2,049	2,066	0.1	20,273	102
Spain - Espagne	46,815,915	23,104,350	23,711,560	46,562	46,549	0.0	505,980	92
Sweden - Suède	9,482,855	4,726,834	4,756,021	9,378	10,058	1.0	438,574	23
Switzerland - Suisse	8,035,391	3,973,280	4,062,111	7,825	8,420	1.0	41,291	204
TFYR of Macedonia - L'ex-R. y. de Macédoine	2,022,547	1,015,377	1,007,170	2,055	2,075	0.1	25,713	81
Ukraine	48,240,902	22,316,317	25,924,585	45,871	42,316	-1.2	603,500	70
United Kingdom of Great Britain and Northern Ireland	63,379,787	31,126,054	32,253,733	62,759	65,809	0.7	242,495	271

The Demand of product is also influenced by the area where the population live: in Rural, Urban or in intermediate area.
In the OECD Factbook is available the important information about Population migration and its distribution by area

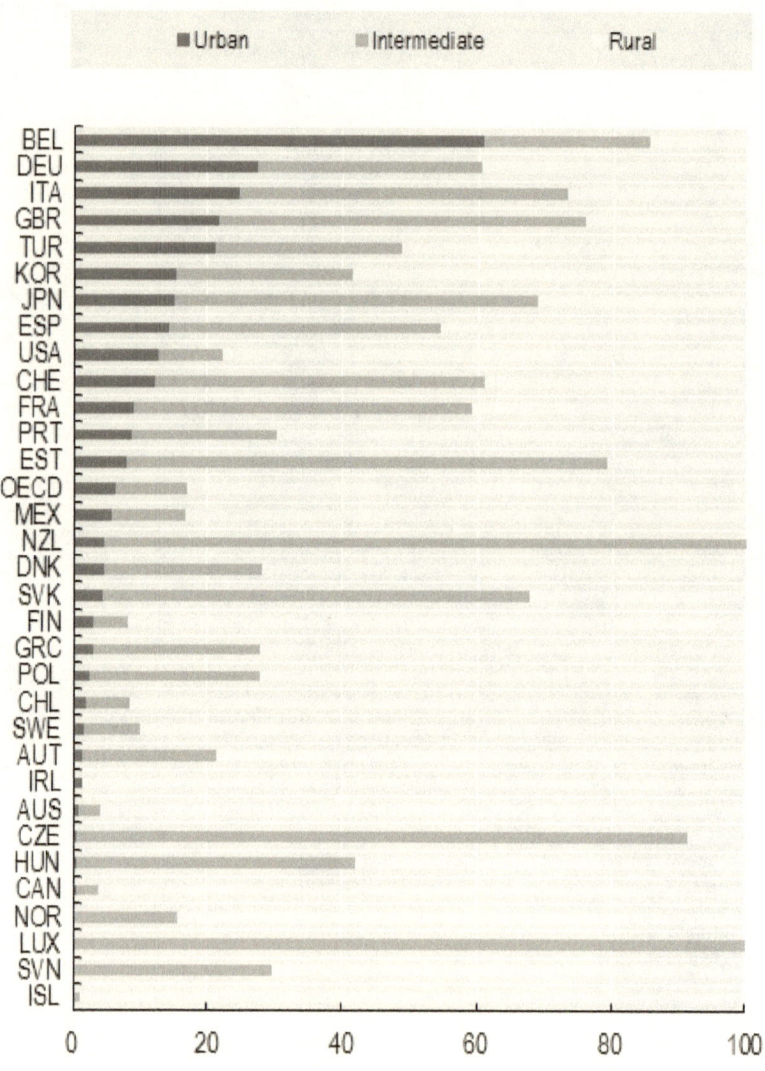

The successful strategy for business growth

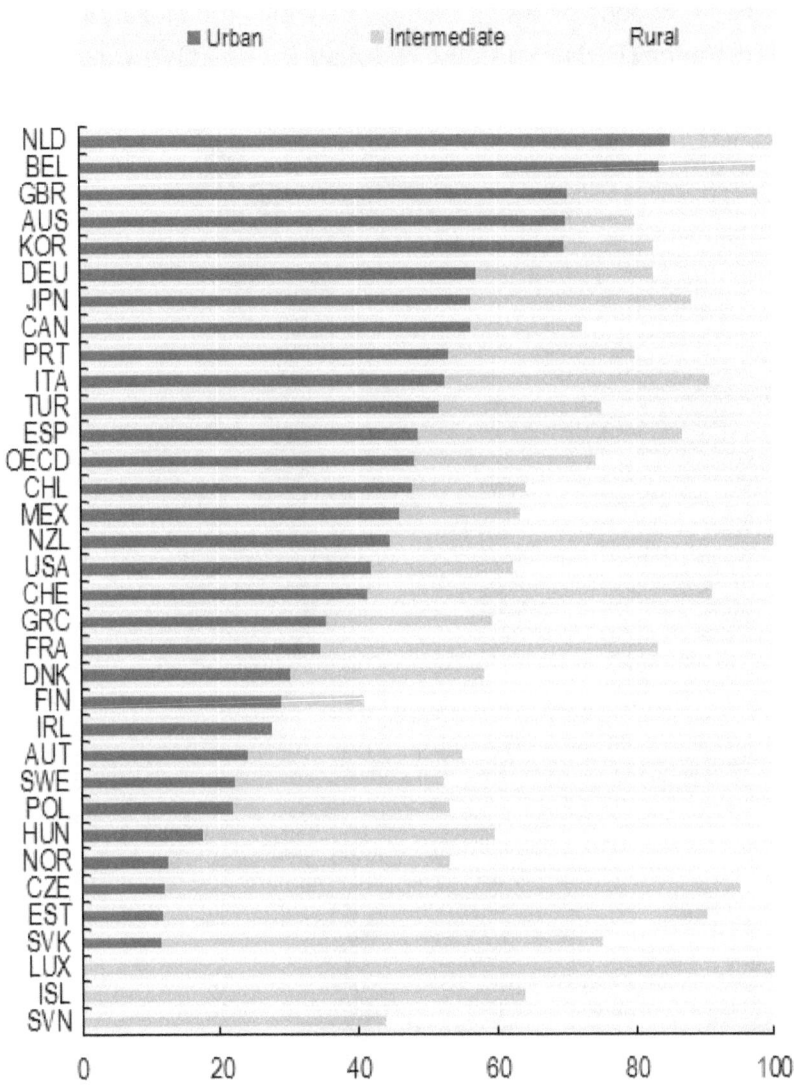

Source: OECD Factbook, percentage, 2014.

It is provided below a table showing the **foreign direct investment (FDI)** (Million US dollars). The FDI creates direct, stable and long-lasting links between economies

	Outflows of foreign direct investment					Inflows of foreign direct investment				
	2010	2011	2012	2013	2014	2010	2011	2012	2013	2014
Australia	19 803	1 716	6 737	1 580	2 114	36 442	58 906	58 970	56 946	47 742
Austria	9 585	21 933	13 114	15 565	6 074	2 576	10 625	3 990	5 719	6 428
Belgium		46 413	33 834	23 063	11 611		76 938	6 518	13 678	3 655
Canada	34 721	52 144	53 948	50 521	57 043	28 399	39 667	39 273	70 545	57 376
Chile	10 226	12 470	17 252	9 217	10 994	15 220	16 815	24 924	18 071	20 820
Czech Republic	1 168	- 328	1 794	4 021	- 529	6 147	2 323	8 000	3 641	5 908
Denmark	1 382	11 278	7 359	9 534	12 984	-9 167	11 488	418	- 742	3 859
Estonia	159	-1 476	1 032	431	- 230	1 453	978	1 558	546	507
Finland				-2 686	- 926				-6 609	15 726
France	48 158	51 462	31 574	24 993	42 871	13 890	31 671	16 985	42 884	15 192
Germany			34 313	104 230					22 395	-6 175
Greece	1 558	1 774	678	- 785	904	330	1 144	1 741	2 817	1 671
Hungary	1 173	4 713	11 717	1 963	3 472	2 195	6 315	14 427	3 333	7 107
Iceland	-2 368	18	-3 205	460	- 237	245	1 107	1 025	397	441
Ireland			22 573	29 023	43 135			45 276	44 890	31 133
Italy				25 107	26 137				24 268	19 538
Japan	56 276	107 550	122 514	135 745	113 699	-1 252	-1 757	1 732	2 303	2 092
Korea	28 280	29 705	30 632	28 360	30 558	9 497	9 773	9 496	12 767	9 899
Luxembourg				25 278	20 541				15 368	16 740
Mexico	15 050	12 636	22 470	13 138	8 304	26 168	23 328	19 492	44 886	24 154
Netherlands	68 363	34 818	6 174	68 856	48 046	-7 185	24 391	20 121	39 026	36 568
New Zealand	716	2 524	- 457	524	71	- 61	4 222	3 396	1 831	2 493
Norway	30 520	14 412	27 536	8 152	21 478	21 238	10 895	26 750	1 608	10 140
Poland	6 149	1 028	2 905	1 488	1 975	12 800	15 953	12 441	3 626	12 532
Portugal	-9 956	13 917	-9 869	- 139	3 138	1 507	5 997	8 337	1 659	5 594
Slovak Republic				- 313	- 123				- 604	- 332
Slovenia	- 19	200	- 258	- 214	264	106	1 088	339	- 151	1 061
Spain				11 771	31 613				27 551	20 314
Sweden	20 364	29 912	28 977	29 074	13 994	141	12 946	16 349	3 673	10 697
Switzerland	73 827	44 084	53 153	10 237	16 819	17 509	24 397	25 844	-22 553	21 942
Turkey	1 469	2 330	4 106	3 525	6 656	9 086	16 136	13 283	12 355	12 198
United Kingdom	48 075	95 577	20 769	-18 770	-81 854	58 180	42 196	55 626	47 589	52 478
United States	301 080	419 061	339 694	328 628	336 935	205 850	236 068	193 795	216 587	111 577
Brazil	16 426	3 850	8 017	13 352	26 042	53 345	71 539	76 111	80 843	96 895
China	57 954	48 421	64 963	72 971	80 418	243 703	280 072	241 214	290 928	289 097
India	15 968	12 608	8 553	1 766	9 951	27 397	36 499	23 996	28 153	33 870
Indonesia	2 664	7 713	5 422	6 652	7 077	13 771	19 241	19 138	18 817	23 039
Russian Federation	41 116	48 635	28 423	70 685	63 513	31 668	36 868	30 188	53 397	30 011
South Africa	- 84	- 229	2 885	6 646	6 939	4 014	3 783	4 403	8 296	5 714

TEN THINGS

You should consider before entering a new market

1. Choose the right Country, with strong Demand and weak supply
2. Check the costs to cover the shipping, insurance, import duties, foreign taxes such as VAT , overseas distribution and storage.
3. Analyze the local competition
4. Know the customers: their investment appetite, their behavior
5. Decide on the best business model: to establish a new local company with local manpower or to use or local distributors
6. Choose the right local partner
7. Prepare a plan: export budget, marketing plan, sales targets, expected return on investment
8. Know the law and regulatory procedures
9. Draft a contractual agreement with your local partner
10. Begin with the right long term attitude

There are many economic indicators created by different sources in both the private and public sector: for example, the Bureau of Labor Statistics, which is the research arm of the U.S. Department of Labor, compiles data on prices, employment and unemployment, work conditions, and productivity. The price report contains information about inflation, import and export prices, and consumer spending.

However for the scope of your strategic feasibility plan, only a selection of them is shown below.

The main economic indicators to be mandatorily analyzed are the following ones:

Gross domestic product (GDP)

Gross domestic product (GDP) is the monetary value of all the finished goods and services produced in a Country in a specific time period. It defines the economic production and growth of the selected Region.

When GDP growth is strong, firms hire more workers and can afford to pay higher salaries and wages, which leads to more spending by consumers on goods and services

In a simple way, GDP is a measurement of a nation's overall economic activity.

Businesses can use GDP as a guide to decide how best to expand or contract their production and other business activities in the future

Investors can use GDP since it provides a framework for investment decision-making

If the GDP has grown since the last year, a company may take the growth as a positive sign and hire more employees, expand its operations, increase the salaries, increase its marketing expenses, build a new factory or purchase more raw materials for production.

However a drop in the GDP value might block the firms on expanding their operations. Instead, many will concentrate on survival, affecting the employees' lifestyle and spending propulsion and therefore the overall customer confidence.

> **KEY NOTE**
>
> If your Selected Region is currently experiencing general growth of GDP per capita, a new phase of growing economy, demographic growth and therefore an increased demand of product is expected.

Nominal vs. Real GDP

Considering that GDP is based on a monetary value of an economy's output, it is subject to the inflationary value
Over a period of time, prices typically tend to rise up and this is reflected in the GDP.
Therefore, just by looking at an economy's GDP that can be sourced online, it is difficult to tell whether the GDP went up as a result of production expanding in the economy or because prices escalated.

This is why is important to identify and study the GDP that has been adjusted by the inflation, the so called real-GDP, rather than the nominal-GDP which ignores inflation and deflation.

In this way, it is possible to compare a country's GDP from one year to another and see if there is any real growth.

Nominal GDP is used when comparing different quarters of output within the same year.

Real GDP is used when comparing the GDP of two or more years, because, by removing the effects of inflation, the comparison of the different years focuses solely on volume.

GDP figures as reported to investors are already adjusted for inflation. In other words, if the gross GDP was calculated to be 8% higher than the previous year, but inflation measured 2% over the same period, GDP growth would be reported as 6%, or the net growth over the period.

The main source of the GDP values for each country and Regions is the IMF International Monetary fund website.

Your analysis can start from the overviews of the GDP globally, to narrow it for different region and then countries.

Details of the GDP and additional links will be provided at the end of this chapter.

Consumer Confidence Index (CCI)

The CCI is an indicator designed to measure the financial health, spending power and confidence of the average consumer.

The CCI tells us about the households' plans to make purchases and their overall current and expected economic condition.

Consumer Price Index (CPI)

The US Bureau of Labor Statistics site describes the CPI as follow: "The Consumer Price Indexes (CPI) program produces monthly data on changes in the prices paid by urban consumers for a representative basket of goods and services."
The Consumer Price Index (CPI) is showing the trend of the inflation in a Country and economy.

It uses a "basket of goods" approach that aims to compare a base of products from year to year, focusing on products that are bought and used by consumers on a daily basis, as prices of food and beverage, housing, apparel, transportation, medical care and education.
Many experts consider CPI as the best gauge of inflation available to investors and others. Inflation has an impact on interest rates

> **KEY NOTE**
>
> The CPI is probably the single most important economic indicator available, giving the trend of the inflation of the market.

and many business and investing decisions. An accurate measure of inflation is key to decision makers in formulating their plans.

Consumer Credit Report

Consumer Credit Report shows the outstanding balances for:
- Commercial banks
- Finance companies
- Federal government & Sallie Mae
- Non-financial businesses

Consumer credit is important because can affect the consumer confidence and other economic indicators. The release of this data allows investors to see how trends in the job market, trends in the value of homes and sentiment about the economy have impacted consumer spending.

Consumer credit is considered a good indicator of the potential future spending levels seen in the Personal Consumption and Retail Sales reports, and shows the extent to which benchmark interest rates such as the fed funds rate and prime rate have translated themselves at the consumer level (it can take six months to a year for macro interest rates to work their way down to consumers).

Durable Goods Report

Durable goods orders tell investors what to expect from the manufacturing sector, a major component of the economy.

The durable goods report indicator provides data on new orders received by manufacturers of durable goods, which are generally defined as higher-priced capital goods orders with a useful life of three years or more, such as cars and turbines.

The Durable Goods Report is important because businesses and consumers generally place orders for durable goods when they are confident the economy is improving.

A durable goods report showing an increase in orders is a sign that the economy is trending upwards.

Employee Situation Report, or Labor report

The labor report is important to investors and can affect the markets. It provides information regarding wage and job growth. Many analysts consider this the best single measure of the health of the economy.

Existing Home Sales

The Existing Home Sales Report provides the information about the number of sales of existing homes that closed along with average sales prices by geographic region. Existing home sales are considered a leading indicator because higher levels are typically reached when the economy is coming out of a recession.

Factory Orders Report

The report provides the dollar value of factory orders for both durable and non-durable goods. It is an important indicator for investors due to the fact that an increase in factory orders usually shows an economy growth.

Consumers are demanding more goods which require retailers to order more from the suppliers. A possible result of the continued increases in factory orders is the rise of inflation in the short period.

A decrease in factory orders, on the other side, can be an indication that the economy is contracting.

Wholesale Trade Report

The report presents three important statistics: monthly sales, monthly inventories and the inventory to sales ratio.

For instance an increment in the value of the Monthly Wholesale Trade indicator is a positive sign for non-durable industries like beverages and apparel.

When inventories are growing more slowly than sales, manufacturers and distributors will have to boost the production to meet demand.

If sales growth is slower than inventory growth, there will be an excess of supply which could indicate a slowdown in manufacturing activity in coming months.

Because manufacturing is such a large part of GDP, the wholesale-trade data can be a valuable indicator to be considered.

Trade Balance Report

The indicator within the Trade Balance Report that is most well-known is the nominal trade deficit, which represents the current exports minus the current imports. The report also covers trade balances for services, such as financial and informational management, as well as for physical goods.

The balance of trade is to be considered in the analysis in

KEY NOTE

A Country's trade balance is the most important component of their current account, the measurement of their net income on foreign trade.

order to determine the relative strength of the economy of one country versus another.

A country with a large trade deficit is borrowing money to purchase goods and services from other trading partners.

Crude Oil Price

How the Crude oil price affect the economy of the Region

During the past decade, the price of oil has changed from $60 per barrel to a peak of $146 in 2009 and subsequently descended again to below $50 in 2015.

The effect of rising or falling prices can be very different for importing and exporting countries.

From a **customer prospective**, a higher oil price is likely to be connected to the price of gasoline, since gasoline purchases are necessary for most households. When gasoline prices increase, a larger share of households' budgets is likely to be spent on it, which leaves less to spend on other goods and services.

From a **business prospective** there is the addition that if there is a product that must be shipped from place to place, the increment of the cost of the fuel will have an higher impact on the business itself.

Higher oil prices tend to make production more expensive for businesses, just as they make it more expensive for households to do the things they normally do.

On a **macroeconomic** level **Oil price increases** are generally thought to increase inflation and reduce economic growth. In terms of inflation, oil prices directly affect the prices of goods made with petroleum products. As mentioned above, oil prices indirectly affect costs such as transportation, manufacturing, and heating.

The increase in these costs can in turn affect the prices of a variety of goods and services, as producers may pass production costs on to consumers. The extent to which oil price increases lead to consumption price increases depends on how important oil is for the production of a given type of good or service.
High oil prices can reduce demand for other goods because they reduce the overall wealth of businesses and households.
The extra payment that the consumers make to foreign oil producers can now no longer be spent on other kinds of consumption goods.

Oil price decrease has these major consequences:
- Increase in the global demand for goods and services
- Benefit for Western and European economies
- Reduction in commodity price
- **Oil importing countries**: reduction of the medium-term inflation. The Central banks might respond with additional monetary policy to support the growth and might reduce the fiscal pressure
- **Oil exporting countries**: lower oil prices might reduce the economic activity
- **Developing countries**: benefit from the decline in the energy input costs
- Lower oil prices reduce energy costs, affecting the transportation, manufacturing costs, agricultural sectors.

the global literature gives evidence that political decision making initiatives play important role for choosing the source of energy.

REMEMBER

The "real" oil price is calculated by dividing the price of oil by the GDP deflator. This removes the effect of inflation and provides a more accurate sense of what is happening to the price of the commodity itself. Real oil price allows comparing oil prices year-by-year

The below chart shows the trend of the oil prices since 1946. The effective cost of oil increased in the 1860s as well as the 1970s, correlating with major events such as oil boom and the oil embargo of 1973. Price drops correspond to new sources of oil, including the beginning of Russian exports. Some of the more significant events in the oil price history are the 1967 Oil Embargo, 1973 oil crisis, 1979 energy crisis, 1980s oil glut, and Oil price increase of 1990.

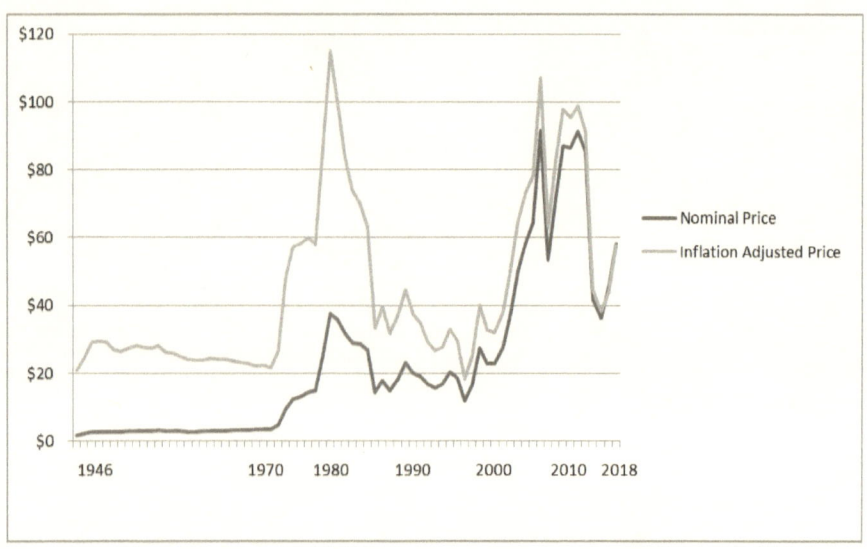

Crude oil prices in history line 1946-2018 (in $/Barrel) – annual average

TO READ MORE

- To read more about supply and demand pressures on the world market for oil, consult the Energy Outlook provided by the U.S. Energy Information Administration: www.eia.gov/analysis/
- To read more about which Countries are the winner or losers in the falling oil price: www.bbc.com/news/business-29643612
- Impact of lower oil prices on Asian economies, consult: www.bangkokpost.com/business/news/464181/impact-of-lower-oil-prices-on-asian-economies
- To read more about what are the possible causes and consequences of higher oil prices on the overall economy: www.frbsf.org/education/publications/doctor-econ/2007/november/oil-prices-impact-economy/
- To read more about how oil price rise impacts economy, markets and your money, consult: economictimes.indiatimes.com/articleshow/64328963.cms?from=mdr&utm_source=contentofinterest&utm_medium=text&utm_campaign=cppst
- To read more on how does the changing price of oil affect your economy, now and potentially in the f uture, consult: www.advancedmanagement.net/article/2015/08/how-does-changing-price-oil-affect-your-economy-now-and-potentially-future

GDP Values

The values of the Real GDP per Country and World Regions are shown below for your information and analysis.
Source: IMF International monetary found

World Regions:

Real GDP growth (Annual percent change)	2012	2013	2014	2015	2016	2017	2018	2019	2020	2021
								Forecast	Forecast	Forecast
Africa (Region)	6.8	3.8	4	3.4	2.1	3.5	3.4	3.9	4	4
Asia and Pacific	5.7	5.9	5.6	5.6	5.3	5.7	5.5	5.2	5.3	5.3
Australia and New Zealand	3.7	2.2	2.7	2.7	2.8	2.3	3.2	2.8	2.7	2.7
Central America	5	3.9	4.1	4.2	3.8	3.7	2.8	3.8	4	3.9
Central Asia and the Caucasus	5.3	7.8	5.1	5	2.9	6.2	3.6	1.7	3.1	2.9
East Asia	5.8	6	5.5	5.3	5.2	5.6	5.3	5	5	4.9
Eastern Europe	2.3	1.6	1.2	-0.4	1.2	2.8	2.8	2.5	2.4	2.2
Europe	0.4	0.6	1.6	1.4	1.7	2.5	2.2	2	1.9	1.8
Middle East (Region)	2.7	2.9	3	1.9	5.9	0.7	1.3	1.9	2.5	2.5
North Africa	12.1	1.4	1.9	3.7	3.2	4.9	4.3	4.5	4.3	4.3
Middle East and North Africa	4.9	2.4	2.7	2.4	5.2	1.8	2	2.5	2.9	3
North America	2.3	1.8	2.5	2.8	1.7	2.2	2.7	2.5	1.9	1.8
South America	2.6	3.3	0.6	-1.1	-2.4	0.7	0.6	1.9	2.5	2.5
Southeast Asia	6.1	5.2	4.7	4.8	4.8	5.3	5.2	5.1	5.1	5.2
Commonwealth of Independent States	3.7	2.5	1.1	-1.9	0.4	2.1	2.3	2.4	2.4	2.3
Emerging and Developing Asia	7	6.9	6.8	6.8	6.5	6.5	6.5	6.3	6.4	6.3
Emerging market and developing economie	5.3	5.1	4.7	4.3	4.4	4.7	4.7	4.7	4.9	4.9
Euro area	-0.9	-0.2	1.4	2.1	1.9	2.4	2	1.9	1.7	1.6
European Union	-0.3	0.3	1.9	2.4	2	2.7	2.2	2	1.8	1.7
Latin America and the Caribbean	2.9	2.9	1.3	0.3	-0.6	1.3	1.2	2.2	2.7	2.7
Major advanced economies (G7)	1.4	1.5	1.9	2.1	1.5	2.1	2.2	2	1.5	1.5
World	3.5	3.5	3.6	3.5	3.3	3.7	3.7	3.7	3.7	3.6

The successful strategy for business growth

Europe:

Real GDP growth (Annual percent change)	2012	2013	2014	2015	2016	2017	2018	2019	2020	2021
								Forecast	Forecast	Forecast
Albania	1.4	1	1.8	2.2	3.4	3.8	4	3.7	3.9	3.9
Austria	0.7	0	0.8	1.1	1.5	3	2.8	2.2	1.6	1.5
Belgium	0.2	0.2	1.3	1.4	1.4	1.7	1.5	1.5	1.5	1.5
Czech Republic	-0.8	-0.5	2.7	5.3	2.5	4.3	3.1	3	2.5	2.5
Denmark	0.2	0.9	1.6	1.6	2	2.3	2	1.9	1.8	1.8
Finland	-1.4	-0.8	-0.6	0.1	2.5	2.8	2.6	1.8	1.6	1.2
France	0.3	0.6	1	1	1.1	2.3	1.6	1.6	1.6	1.6
Germany	0.7	0.6	2.2	1.5	2.2	2.5	1.9	1.9	1.6	1.5
Greece	-7.3	-3.2	0.7	-0.3	-0.2	1.4	2	2.4	2.2	1.6
Italy	-2.8	-1.7	0.1	1	0.9	1.5	1.2	1	0.9	0.8
Luxembourg	-0.4	3.7	5.8	2.9	3.1	2.3	4	3.5	3.3	3.2
Malta	2.7	4.6	8.2	9.5	5.2	6.7	5.7	4.6	4	3.5
Netherlands	-1	-0.1	1.4	2	2.2	2.9	2.8	2.6	2.3	2.1
Norway	2.7	1	2	2	1.1	1.9	2.1	2.1	1.9	1.9
Poland	1.6	1.4	3.3	3.8	3	4.6	4.4	3.5	3	2.8
Portugal	-4	-1.1	0.9	1.8	1.6	2.7	2.3	1.8	1.5	1.4
Romania	1.2	3.5	3.4	3.9	4.8	6.9	4	3.4	3.3	3.2
Russian Federation	3.7	1.8	0.7	-2.5	-0.2	1.5	1.7	1.8	1.8	1.6
Serbia	-1	2.6	-1.8	0.8	2.8	1.9	4	3.5	4	4
Slovak Republic	1.7	1.5	2.8	3.9	3.3	3.4	3.9	4.1	3.8	3.7
Slovenia	-2.7	-1.1	3	2.3	3.1	5	4.5	3.4	2.8	2.6
Spain	-2.9	-1.7	1.4	3.6	3.2	3	2.7	2.2	1.9	1.7
Sweden	-0.3	1.2	2.6	4.5	2.7	2.1	2.4	2.2	2	2
Switzerland	1	1.9	2.5	1.3	1.6	1.7	3	1.8	1.7	1.7
United Kingdom	1.4	2	2.9	2.3	1.8	1.7	1.4	1.5	1.5	1.6
World	3.5	3.5	3.6	3.5	3.3	3.7	3.7	3.7	3.7	3.6

Americas:

Real GDP growth (Annual percent change)	2012	2013	2014	2015	2016	2017	2018	2019	2020	2021
								Forecast	Forecast	Forecast
Argentina	-1	2.4	-2.5	2.7	-1.8	2.9	-2.6	-1.6	2.2	2.5
Bolivia	5.1	6.8	5.5	4.9	4.3	4.2	4.3	4.2	3.9	3.8
Brazil	1.9	3	0.5	-3.5	-3.5	1	1.4	2.4	2.3	2.2
Canada	1.7	2.5	2.9	1	1.4	3	2.1	2	1.8	1.8
Chile	5.3	4.1	1.8	2.3	1.3	1.5	4	3.4	3.2	3
Colombia	3.9	4.6	4.7	3	2	1.8	2.8	3.6	3.7	3.6
Costa Rica	4.8	2.3	3.5	3.6	4.2	3.3	3.3	3.3	3.4	3.4
Dominican Republic	2.7	4.9	7.6	7	6.6	4.6	6.4	5	5.2	5
Ecuador	5.6	4.9	3.8	0.1	-1.2	2.4	1.1	0.7	1.3	1.7
Guatemala	3	3.7	4.2	4.1	3.1	2.8	2.8	3.4	3.8	3.7
Honduras	4.1	2.8	3.1	3.8	3.8	4.8	3.5	3.6	3.6	3.6
Jamaica	-0.5	0.2	0.6	0.9	1.5	0.7	1.2	1.5	1.7	2
Mexico	3.6	1.4	2.8	3.3	2.9	2	2.2	2.5	2.7	2.9
Panama	9.2	6.6	6	5.8	5	5.4	4.6	6.8	6	5.5
Paraguay	-0.5	8.4	4.9	3.1	4.3	4.8	4.4	4.2	3.9	3.9
Peru	6	5.8	2.4	3.3	4	2.5	4.1	4.1	4.1	4.1
United States of America	2.2	1.8	2.5	2.9	1.6	2.2	2.9	2.5	1.8	1.7
Uruguay	3.5	4.6	3.2	0.4	1.7	2.7	2	3.2	3.4	3.2
Venezuela	5.6	1.3	-3.9	-6.2	-16.5	-14	-18	-5	-2	-1.5
Caribbean	1.4	3.5	4.4	4.5	3.2	2.6	4.4	3.7	3.9	3.9
Central America	5	3.9	4.1	4.2	3.8	3.7	2.8	3.8	4	3.9
World	3.5	3.5	3.6	3.5	3.3	3.7	3.7	3.7	3.7	3.6

Asia and Oceania:

Real GDP growth (Annual percent change)	2012	2013	2014	2015	2016	2017	2018	2019	2020	2021
								Forecast	Forecast	Forecast
Australia	3.9	2.2	2.6	2.5	2.6	2.2	3.2	2.8	2.7	2.6
Brunei Darussalam	0.9	-2.1	-2.5	-0.4	-2.5	1.3	2.3	5.1	4.3	7.5
Cambodia	7.3	7.4	7.1	7	7	6.9	6.9	6.8	6.5	6.3
China, People's Republic of	7.9	7.8	7.3	6.9	6.7	6.9	6.6	6.2	6.2	6
India	5.5	6.4	7.4	8.2	7.1	6.7	7.3	7.4	7.7	7.7
Indonesia	6	5.6	5	4.9	5	5.1	5.1	5.1	5.2	5.3
Japan	1.5	2	0.4	1.4	1	1.7	1.1	0.9	0.3	0.7
Korea, Republic of	2.3	2.9	3.3	2.8	2.9	3.1	2.8	2.6	2.8	2.8
Malaysia	5.5	4.7	6	5.1	4.2	5.9	4.7	4.6	4.8	4.8
Myanmar	7.3	8.4	8	7	5.9	6.8	6.4	6.8	7	7
Nepal	4.8	4.1	6	3.3	0.6	7.9	6.3	5	4.2	4.2
New Zealand	2.5	2.2	3.2	4.2	4.1	3	3.1	3	3.1	3.1
Philippines	6.7	7.1	6.1	6.1	6.9	6.7	6.5	6.6	6.6	6.8
Singapore	4.1	5.1	3.9	2.2	2.4	3.6	2.9	2.5	2.7	2.7
Taiwan Province of China	2.1	2.2	4	0.8	1.4	2.9	2.7	2.4	2.3	1.9
Thailand	7.2	2.7	1	3	3.3	3.9	4.6	3.9	3.7	3.5
Vietnam	5.2	5.4	6	6.7	6.2	6.8	6.6	6.5	6.5	6.5
Pacific Islands	3.7	3.7	12.1	4.7	1.7	2.7	0.2	3.7	3.2	3.3
World	3.5	3.5	3.6	3.5	3.3	3.7	3.7	3.7	3.7	3.6

Middle East:

Real GDP growth (Annual percent change)	2012	2013	2014	2015	2016	2017	2018	2019	2020	2021
								Forecast	Forecast	Forecast
Bahrain	3.7	5.4	4.4	2.9	3.5	3.8	3.2	2.6	2.5	2.5
Iran	-7.7	-0.3	3.2	-1.6	12.5	3.7	-1.5	-3.6	1.1	1.6
Iraq	13.9	7.6	0.7	2.5	13.1	-2.1	1.5	6.5	3.2	2.7
Kuwait	7.9	0.4	0.6	-1	2.2	-3.3	2.3	4.1	4.1	4
Lebanon	2.8	2.7	2	0.2	1.7	1.5	1	1.4	2	2.4
Oman	9.1	5.1	1.4	4.7	5	-0.9	1.9	5	2.7	3.1
Qatar	4.7	4.4	4	3.7	2.1	1.6	2.7	2.8	2.6	2.7
Saudi Arabia	5.4	2.7	3.7	4.1	1.7	-0.9	2.2	2.4	1.9	2.1
United Arab Emirates	4.5	5.1	4.4	5.1	3	0.8	2.9	3.7	3.6	3.2
World	3.5	3.5	3.6	3.5	3.3	3.7	3.7	3.7	3.7	3.6

Proceeding even further with the analysis, it is recommended to compare the values of the selected country with the values of wider Regions, as the USA or the World.

As example, in the first below graphic is compared the GDP of Italy versus the USA and the World GDP. In the second graphic the GDP of China, USA and Russia are compared.

The successful strategy for business growth

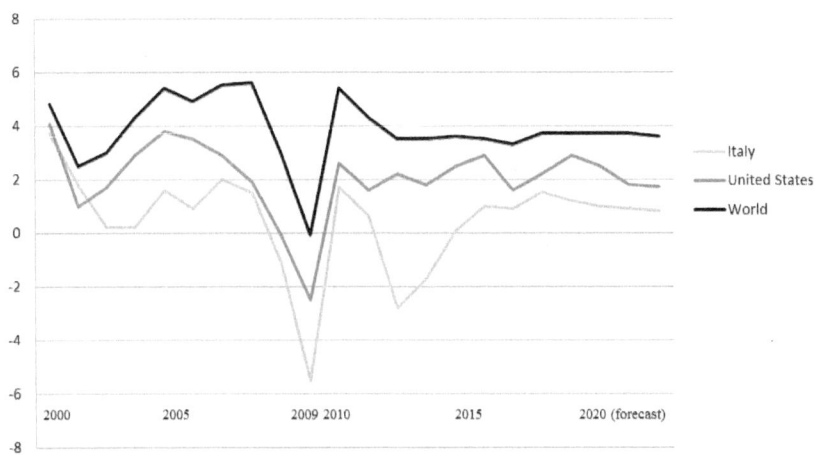

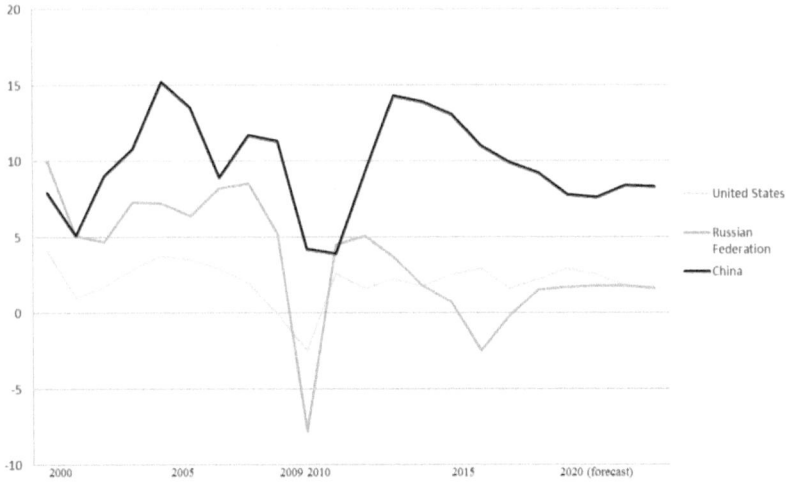

As further example of the information that **must** be collected by the analysis of the GDP, in the following graphics is provided a **breakdown of the GDP by industries of the United Arab Emirates** country for the year 2010- 2011.

The **breakdown of the GDP is a mandatory step to be done because it will be used in the creation of the** appetite index (in the chapter four) and in the correct definition of the statistical region where set up your primary search.

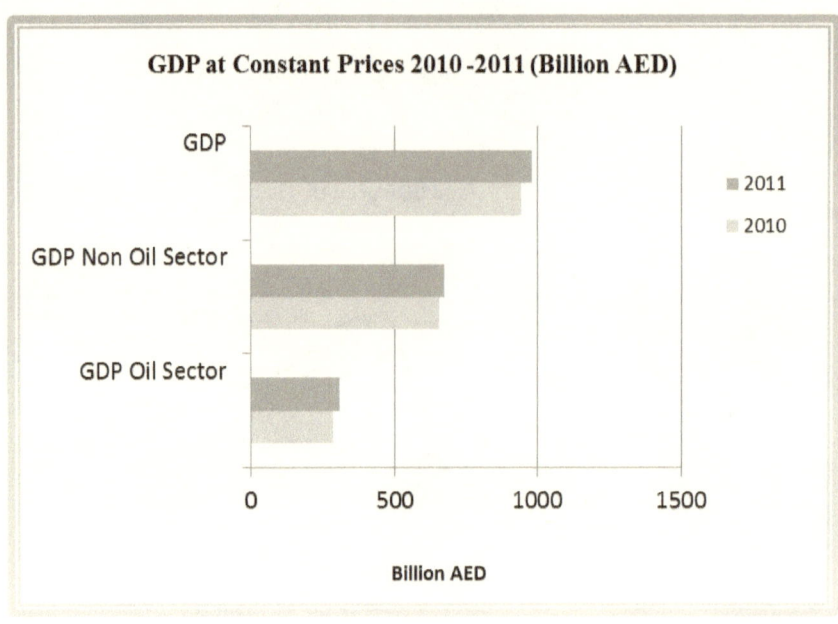

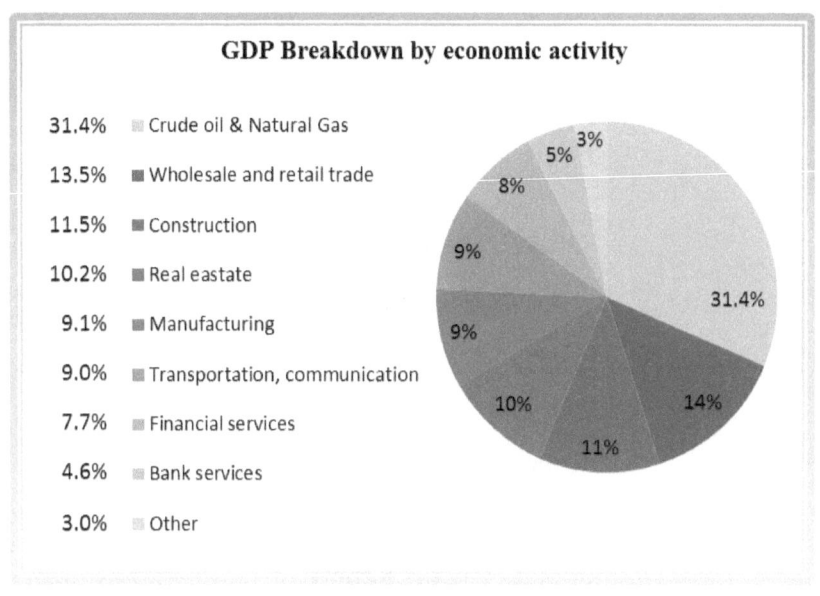

Source: Annual Economic Report – 2012 – UAE Statistic
Department.

ECONOMIC INDICATORS
You should know about the Selected Region

1. Gross Domestic Product (GDP)
2. Consumer Confidence Index (CCI)
3. Consumer Credit Report
4. Durable Goods Report
5. Employee Cost Index (ECI)
6. Employee Situation Report
7. Jobless Claims Report
8. Existing Home Sales
9. Housing Starts
10. Industrial Production
11. Factory Orders Report
12. Money Supply
13. Mutual Fund Flows
14. Non-Manufacturing Report
15. Productivity Report
16. Personal Income and Outlays
17. Producer Price Index (PPI)
18. Purchasing Managers Index (PMI)
19. Retail Sales Report, Wholesale Trade Report
20. Trade Balance Report

CHAPTER THREE

STRATEGIC ANALYSIS
OF THE SELECTED
INDUSTRY

CHAPTER 3

STRATEGIC ANALYSIS OF THE SELECTED INDUSTRY

"No company, small or large, can win over the long run without energized employees who believe in the company mission & goals and understand how to achieve them"

Jack Welch

In this chapter is explained how to carry out the strategic analysis of the Industry to understand the importance and influence of the stakeholders (the key players) and an analysis of the characteristic of your product to be consolidated or improved in order to enter the selected market.

The strategic frameworks used will be:
- Five forces of the Industry impacting on the profitability of the Industry, called Porter's five forces model.
- PEST analysis
- SWOT analysis.

As previously mentioned, even if the reader is familiar with the methods, the author recommends to follow point by point the indications mentioned in the next chapters in order to optimize the primary search and the creation of the appetite index.

INDUSTRY DEFINITION

Which is your Industry, Who is the customer, Value preposition, levels of Strategy

SECONDARY SEARCH

Industry review, supply and demand, Porter 5 Forces, PEST, SWOT, Firm Value Chain, timing market entry, Resources and capabilities, Economic indicators

PRIMARY RESEARCH

Statistical method of research, questionnaire creation

APPETITE INDEX OF CLIENTS AND INVESTORS

Investment conditions and buying conditions.

CONCLUSIONS

Viable Strategy definition, Business models definition

PORTER'S 5 FORCES

Named after Michael Porter (Harvard Business Review, 1979), the model identifies and analyzes five competitive forces that impact on the profitability of every industry, and helps determine an industries weaknesses, strengths and strategy
The framework takes into consideration the following five forces:

- Competitive rivalry in the industry
- potential of new entrants
- bargaining power of suppliers
- bargaining power of customers
- Threat of substitute products.

These forces jointly determine the intensity of industry competition and profitability, and understanding them is important in order to be able to formulate a viable strategy.

Competitive Rivalry

Based on the secondary research carried out on the literature, you will be able at this point to highlight the competitors of the selected Region as follows:

- Competitors with a representative office and operations inside the selected Region. These competitors might have an advantage being in the Market and being closed to the customers on a daily basis.
- the market share of each one of the competitors
- the market position and the key competitive advantages of each one of them.

Threat of new entrants in an Industry

Threats of new entrants depend largely on barriers to entry. Professor Porter identifies six major barriers to entry:

- Economies of scale, or decline in unit costs of the product, which force the entrant to enter on a large scale and risk a strong reaction from firms already in the industry, or accepting a disadvantage of costs if entering on a small scale.
- Product differentiation, or brand identification and customer loyalty.
- Capital requirements for entry; the investment of large capital presents a significant risk.
- Switching cost, or the cost the buyer has to absorb to switch from one supplier to another.
- Access to distribution channels. New entrants have to establish their distribution in a market to secure a space for their product.
- Cost disadvantages independent of scale, whereby established companies already have product technology, access to raw materials, favorable sites, advantages in the form of government subsidies, and experience.

> **KEY NOTE**
>
> Barriers to entry may be natural , created by governments (licensing fees or patents) or by other firms (monopolists)

Barriers to entry are high start-up costs or other obstacles that prevent new competitors from easily entering an industry or area of business.

Barriers to entry benefit existing firms because they protect their revenues and profits.

Threat of Entry of New Competitors is high when:
- Profitability does not require economies of scale
- Products are undifferentiated
- Brand names are not well-known. Low brand awareness
- Initial capital investment is low or easy to be accessed
- Consumer switching costs are low
- Accessing distribution channels is easy
- Proprietary technology is not an issue
- Government policy are not limiting the import of new products

Threat of New Entry is Low if:
- Profitability requires economies of scale
- Products are differentiated
- Brand names are well-known
- Initial capital investment is high
- Consumer switching costs are high
- Accessing distribution channels is difficult
- Location is an issue
- Proprietary technology is an issue
- Government policy create a strong entry barrier

Bargaining power of the supplier

The next step of the analysis will focus the potential suppliers and their bargaining power:
a supplier has got **more power over an industry** if shows long term financial stability and a secure operational plan, if its technology is unique, if there are no substitute products, if their product is essential to the industry, if supplier group exists.

The bargaining power can be influenced by following factors:
- Global economy: global crisis can reduced the trust of the clients on investments opportunities a company needs to work more to acquire the clients and investor's confidence;
- Increased information available online: the buyers will review any available information before its desired product. Thanks to new technologies, each potential Client can easily collect information regarding your competitors, therefore you need to offer a unique service and provide an higher value to attract and retain your existing and new client.

Bargaining power of the buyers

The power of the buyers can be considered strong if can affect the changes in the prices as force prices down, demand higher quality products or services.
Buyers has got more power when they are large-volume buyers, the product is a significant aspect of the buyer's costs or purchases, the products are standard within an industry, there are few changing or switching costs, the buyers earn low profits, potential for backward integration of the buyer group exists, the

product is not essential to the buyer's product, and the buyer has full disclosure about supply, demand, prices, and costs.

Threat of substitution

Substitute products are the natural result of industry competition. A substitute product is a product that can do the same function as the product the industry already produces, at a lower cost. Example of substitute products and investments are for instance the Tourism and tech industries, that are attractive sectors for many investors that might be willing to divert their investment in those sectors and not in your industry and business.

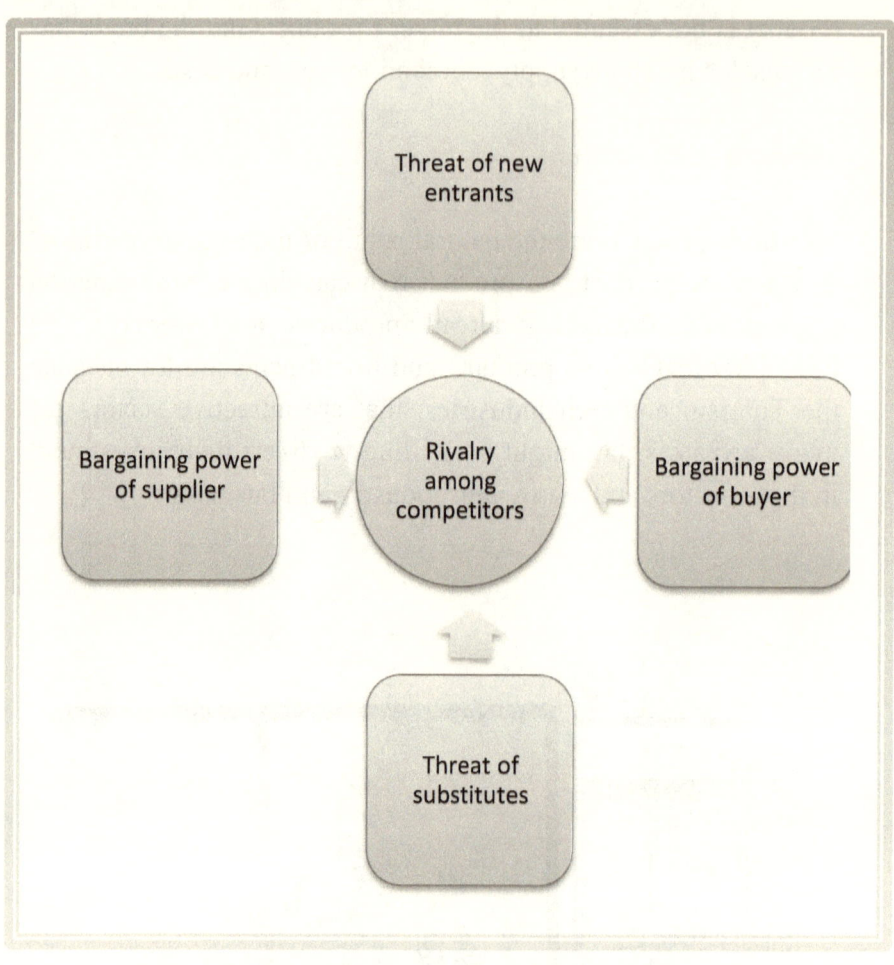

Porter five forces within the selected Industry

We will now present three practical examples of Porter's 5 industry forces: for the Airline industry, for the hotel and hospitality industry, and for the Fitness industry.

Example 1: Airline Industry

Competitive Rivalry
-   Intense rivalry between the airlines in order to achieve the market leadership
-   High rivalry due boosted by the low cost airlines
-   The clients can easily switch between the airlines

Threat of new entry
-   High bureaucracy involved in setting up a new airlines
-   Economies of scale

Threat of substitution
-   Substitute transportation: road, high speed train, marine.
-   Cost to change to the train is less expensive

Supplier power
-   Labor cost might impact for the 40% of the total cost
-   Presence of a duopoly: Boeing and Airbus
-   No control towards the raising of the fuel and oil price

Buyer power
-   The power of the buyers, the passengers, has increased due to the online booking
-   Passengers are price sensitive

Example 2: Hotel Industry

Competitive Rivalry
- Intense rivalry to acquire market leadership
- High number of competitors
- Occupancy rate
- Industry profitability

Threat of new entry
- International chains entering in attractive domestic market
- New entrepreneurial players

Threat of substitution
- Airbnb business
- Videocalling and no need to carry out a business trip

Supplier power
- Labor cost
- Availability of skilled management
- Food, beverage, utility costs

Buyer power
- online booking
- Corporate agreements that reduce the profit per room

Example 3: Fitness Industry

Competitive Rivalry
- Intense rivalry because the population is resident in a small area

Threat of new entry
- Smaller new gym, with less overhead costs
- high capital costs, government regulations and licensing, or professional knowledge

Threat of substitution
- Different working out programs, according to the trend (bodybuilding, fitness, bodypump, crossfit, aerobic, zumba)

Supplier power
- Rental cost (landlord), equipment leasing companies, any business that supplies you with goods or services and impact your operation and overhead costs

Buyer power
- The customers are price sensitive
- The customers change workout taste according to the trend of the moment (eg. CrossFit)

PEST Analysis

After having defined the Five forces of Porter, it is now time to carry out the PEST analysis.

The PEST analysis is commonly defined as the analysis carried out considering the political-legal, economic, socio-cultural and technological factors that can affect Firm long-term plans.

Two additional factors might be also added to the analysis, environmental and legal, to make a broader PESTEL analysis, but these factors are not required to be separated into individual categorical analysis as they can easily be merged within the other categories.

Remember that the sequence of the analysis has to be followed in order for the Porter's five forces to support you in better defining the PEST analysis.

Political analysis

Information about political situation in the selected Region can be found easily in the online literature. A key note would be to include studies of IMF (International Monetary Founds) on a global and local level in order to observe whether there is a growing commitment from the Government to put policies and public programs in place in order to encourage the growth of your specific industry and line of business.

Economic analysis

The economic analysis will not only touch the trend of the economy in the regions, as growth or recession, but it need to study also macroeconomic factors and Index that can have a positive or negative relationship in your market entry, such as:

- Interest rate: an high interest rate reflects the relative scarcity of financing, and the tendency to reduce investments and is affecting the borrowing/lending from a bank institute.
- Inflation rate
- Real GDP growth **(obtained by the study of the economic indicators)**
- Growth or recession cycle

Technological analysis

The expansion of your product in a new market will be also possible by the technological innovation that is impacting on the cost reduction of the manufacturing of it, and therefore on the increment of its profit.

Technical factors to be analyzed are for example: automated processes in the industry, rate of innovation, changes in technology incentives, Internet usage.

Social analysis

The population growth experienced by your region along with social stability is expected to result in growth in demand for food, consumer goods, fuel, energy for the living and energy to produce the goods.

A positive relationship between Social stability, population growth and raise in product demand is therefore expected.

Social factors to be studied are among the following ones: social and ethnic customs, age of the populations, religious orientation, race and ethnicity, education, economic status, shift in educational needs and changing career attitudes.

"You've got everything we're looking for. Almost."

Social Factors
Source: www.breakthroughvisuals.com

When looking at opportunities and threats, PEST analysis can help to ensure that you don't overlook external factors, such as new government regulations or technological changes.

Political

- Government commitment
- political stability and economic growth.
- Governmental control over the
   investments in new sectors
- tax policy

Economical

- interest rates
- energy prices
- capital surplus
- Real GDP
- inflation
- unemployment rate

Social

- Population growth
- age distribution
- life style attitude
- Growing awareness global issues
- level of instruction
- global influence

Technological

- technological innovation impactiong on cost reduction
   and profit improvement
- R&D activity
- automation
-research funding

PEST analysis

SWOT Analysis

Based on Porter's Five Forces of the Industry and the results of the PEST analysis, in this section is illustrated the SWOT strategic framework that is used to evaluate the strengths, weaknesses, opportunities and the threats involved in your business model.

Strengths

Highlight at this point the analysis the strengths of your Brand, of your product, of your Company, strengths that can be exploited in order for you to enter in the new market.

Examples of strengths could be the followings:
- Brand recognition
- Network of your Group
- Business references
- Clear and exact strategic positioning of your Company

> **KEY NOTE**
>
> Strengths and weaknesses are often internal to your organization, while opportunities and threats generally relate to external factors.

To help you to define additional strengths, answer to the following questions:
- What advantages does your Firm have?
- What do you do better than the competitors?
- What unique resources you have?
- What do people in your market see as your strengths?
- **What is your organization's Unique Selling Proposition (USP)?**

Weaknesses

In order to define the weaknesses of your product or brand, it is necessary to look back at the Porter's Five Forces and the PEST analysis to check how the product will fit in the new selected market.

Examples of weaknesses are:
- weak marketing actions and marketing tools, not covering the full range suggested by the IMC Integrated marketing communication frameworks
- unclear brand definition
- unclear unique selling point.

Additional questions to be asked to identify the weaknesses are:
- How can the Value chain be improved?
- Which internal operations generate a cost lost?
- What should you avoid?
- What are people in your market likely to see as weaknesses?
- What factors make lose you sales?

Opportunities

The opportunities presented to your company in the exploitation of the Selected Region need to be analyzed among both macroeconomic than local figures.

Examples of them are:
- the global shift to a low-carbon economy
- a new phase of political support
- tax exemptions projection of future product demand
- demographic and GDP growth values
- Changes in technology and markets

- Changes in government policy related to your field.
- Changes in social patterns, population profiles, lifestyle

Threats

To analyze the Threats for your future development and success in the selected Region the analysis has to be based this time on:
- Existing partnership between competitors or organizations,
- Difficulty to achieve capitals
- market lobbies
- the threat of the governmental policies
- **Rating agencies values** that instead of protecting investors from risks may tend to disadvantage investments. The dependence on ratings agencies also acts as a particular barrier to cross-border investment in the developing world, where few countries and even fewer utilities are rated as investment-grade

Additional questions to be asked to identify the threats are:
- What obstacles do you face?
- What are your competitors doing?
- Are quality standards for your products or services changing?
- Is changing technology threatening your position?
- Do you have bad debt or cash-flow problems?

Strength	**Opportunities**
Brand recognition Successful business model Clear strategic positioning Recognized commitment and reputation	Economy growth New phase of political support Growing investment
SWOT	
Lack of networking low number of Assets Weak marketing actons not covering the full range of activities suggested by the IMC Integrated marketing communication	Partnership between competitors Political instability High inflation Investments towards nearest Countries or products or assets
Weaknesses	**Threats**

SWOT analysis

TO READ MORE

To read more about the **Countries in which is easy to do business**, an useful resource is the World Bank doing business report, that ranks 190 countries based on how easy is to do business there, taking into account trading regulations, property rights, the availability of credit, contract enforcement, and many other factors:

- www.worldbank.org/content/dam/doingBusiness/media/Annual-Reports/English/DB2019-report_web-version.pdf

To read more about the **industry 5 forces of Porter**, the PEST analysis and the SWOT analysis, useful resources are:

- www.referenceforbusiness.com/management/Or-Pr/Porter-s-5-Forces-Model.html
- www.allassignmenthelp.com/blog/5-best-and-practical-pestle-analysis-examples-to-know/
- www.marketingtutor.net/technological-factors-affect-business/

RESOURCES AND CAPABILITIES

"Strategy is simply resource allocation. Strategy means making clear cut choices about how to compete. You cannot be everything to everybody, no matter what the size of your business"

Jack Welch

"Strategy is a pattern of resource allocation that enables firms to maintain or improve their performance."

Jay Barney
Gaining and Sustaining Competitive Advantage

This section will present the methodology to analyze the resources which an organization owns. Resources can be physical, tangible and human. The resources and capabilities are the core of the competitive advantage of the organization.

"No Shakespeare plays yet, but we have gotten some pretty good blog posts."

Firm value chain

The concept of the Value chain of a Company was firstly introduced and described by Professor Michael Porter in his popular book *Competitive Advantage: Creating and sustaining superior performance*

The model has to be used to identify which activities are contributing to a competitive advantage and which were not.

The approach involves breaking down the firm into five 'primary' and four 'support' activities, and then looking at each to see if they give a cost advantage or quality advantage.

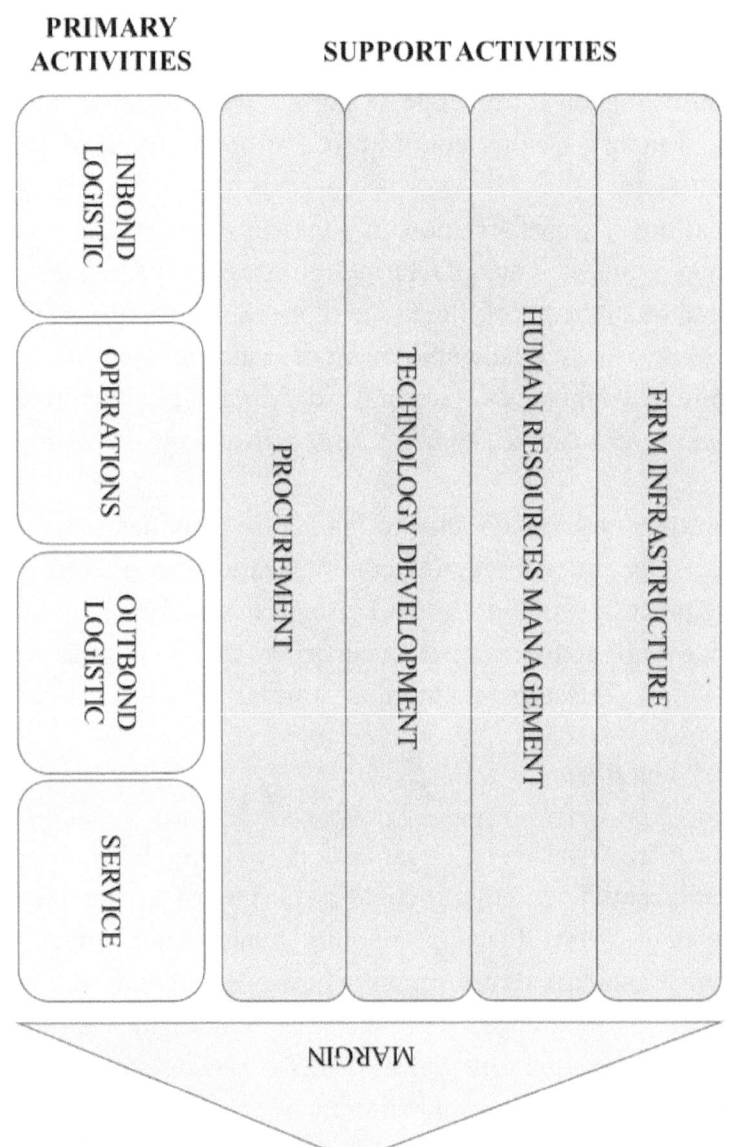

Primary activities

- **Inbound logistics** - receiving, storing and handling raw material inputs. Quality control process, optimization of the stock system.
- **Operations** - transformation of the raw materials into finished goods; manufacturing process; maintenance process; quality control; the usage of machines and the latest technology, as well the employment of skilled manpower.
- **Outbound logistics** - storing, distributing, delivering finished goods to customers; order handling; invoicing process.
- **Marketing and sales** – all the marketing activities part of the IMC integrated marketing communication process; order taking process, promotions, market and sales analysis.
- **Service** - all activities that occur after the sale, such as installation, education and training, warranty.

Secondary activities

- **Firm infrastructure** - Organization of the Firm. For example centralized buying could result in cost savings due to higher discounts. Legal, accounting, financial department.
- **Human resources development** - how people contribute to competitive advantage. For example employing expert buyers and experiences Sales Director could exploit the business better than the competitors.
- **Technology development** - how the firm uses the latest technology; product and process design, engineering, R&D
- **Procurement** - purchasing, but not just limited to materials; funding, subcontracting.

CHAPTER FOUR

THE PRIMARY RESEARCH

&

THE APPETITE INDEX

OF CLIENT AND INVESTORS

CHAPTER 4

THE PRIMARY RESEARCH METHOD

"Success is 1% inspiration, 99% perspiration "

Thomas A. Edison

Following the detailed analysis carried so far regarding the supply and demand on both global and local scale, this chapter will guide you in carrying out the **primary research** which has to be designed as a survey in order to take form the Market the following unique up-to-date information:

• Understanding the appetite of the prospect Clients or investors (individual, institutional and private companies) in buying the product offered by your Company;

> ### KEY NOTE
>
> The primary research shows results which are not available in the literature, therefore it shows precious information which can be used as guidance to expand your operation within the Selected Region.

• Defining the reasons behind the investment and buying decisions of the surveyed customers when your product is proposed them.

The findings of the survey will be compared and analyzed against findings of the Industry and literature analysis.

INDUSTRY DEFINITION

Which is your Industry, Who is the customer, Value preposition, levels of Strategy

SECONDARY SEARCH

Industry review, supply and demand, Porter 5 Forces, PEST, SWOT, Firm Value Chain, timing market entry, Resources and capabilities, Economic indicators

PRIMARY RESEARCH

Statistical method of research, questionnaire creation

APPETITE INDEX OF CLIENTS AND INVESTORS

Investment conditions and buying conditions.

CONCLUSIONS

Viable Strategy definition, Business models definition

Approach

The survey has to be carried out in the correct *reference market* and in the correct *selected statistical sample*, using the right questions.

The following are identified as **key steps**:

1. **Survey questionnaire**.
   Plan and design a questionnaire writing questions in a fennel way, starting from the most generic to the most detailed one, and asking information about how the respondent sees the industry, see the competitors, under which conditions would be interest in buying your product or invest in your Company.

2. Selection of the **Reference market** and selection of the **statistical sample within the universe:**
   - The survey should be sent to companies, potential clients or potential investors belonging to the selected statistical sample of the reference market **that are impacting for the higher percentage on the creation of the GDP or wealth of the Region**.
   A simple example of it will be shown in the next pages.
   - The statistical sample, basically the People to be interviewed, should be based on business lists showing how they impact on the creation of the wealth or GDP of the Regions. A good source of it is the **FORBES list** that shows the companies, CEO, Entrepreneurs and Investor divided by Industry and Regions.

3. **Delivery of the questionnaire**: In order to reach the decision maker within the targeted companies and in the market segment, an invitations to complete the surveys has to be sent to the CEOs,CFOs, the investment Managers, private citizens and Industry influencer through the professional social media site like LinkedIn, or through marketing focus group, in order to achieve a higher response and therefore increase the responding sample size.

   The online survey should be created to be completed within few minutes, in the aim to increase the size of the responding sample.

4. **Responses**: The Response rate to the survey will help you to generate the Appetite Index, described at the end of this chapter.

Advantages of the Primary Research

- The data collected is up to date and is accurate. Also, this research method can be customized to suit personal requirements and needs of organizations or businesses.
- Primary research focuses mainly on your needs and problems which mean entire attention is directed to find solution to a specific question or issue.
- Data collected can be controlled. Primary research gives a means to control how data is collected, used, and which information out of it you need to plan your strategy.

Disadvantages of the Primary Research

- One of the major disadvantages of primary research is that can be quite expensive to conduct, in terms of cost per hour of the manpower, cost to hire an outsourced marketing firm.
- time-consuming. Conducting interviews, sending and receiving online surveys need investing time for the process to work. Moreover, evaluating results and applying the findings to improve product or service will need additional working time.
- Just using one primary research method may not be enough. In such cases, use of more than one method is required and this might increase both times required to conduct research and the cost associated with it.

Justification of the statistical method of research

In the below section is described the justification for the execution of the survey within the Selected Region and under which conditions has to be selected the reference market and the statistical sample within the universe.

The selection of the **reference market** of the survey can been carried out based on the following rational:

The IMF following statement: "IMF estimates indicate that a mounting current account surplus in a country is as a proportion of the GDP (On the other hand, if an economy is running a current account surplus it is absorbing less than that it is producing. This means it is saving. As the economy is open, this saving is being invested abroad and thus foreign assets are being created."

Therefore, the selected reference market of the survey includes the sectors that are impacting the most on the creation of the GDP.

Practical Example:

The analysis of the GDP of the selected Region carried out in the previous chapters and its split down into main subsectors (as financial services, the manufacturing sub-sector, the Construction sector, agriculture or service sectors.) had provide you an understanding of which Sector is impacting the most in the GDP creation in the Region, and consequently in which industry develop the primary search.

For instance, let's analyze the breakdown of the GDP of the United Arab Emirates, provided by the official website of the economic department of the UAE. Other source of information about the GDP composition can be found in the IMF (International Monetary Fund) website, or in the Regional Chamber of commerce websites and report.

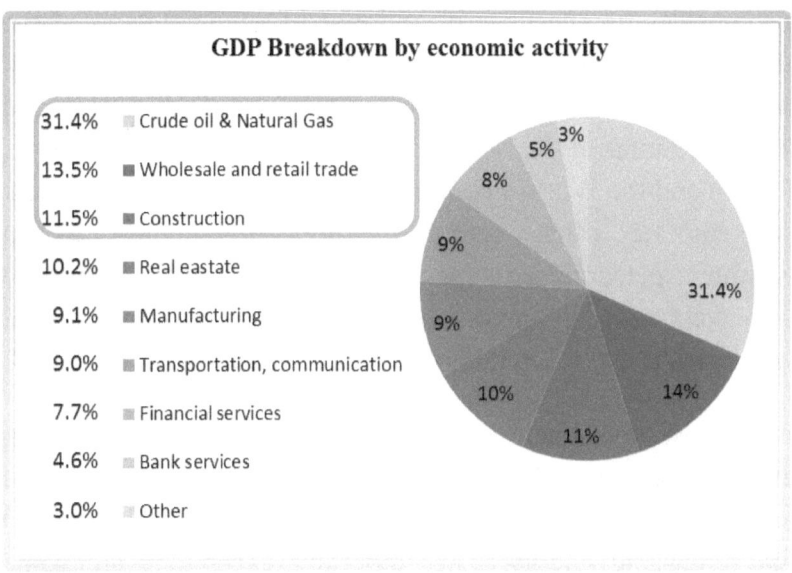

As we can see the Industries impacting in the creation of the GDP of the UAE Regions are the Oil Industry (31,4%), The trade Industry (13,5%) and the Construction Industry (11,5%).

The **reference market** of the primary search will include the following Professionals:

- Main Professionals belonging to these 3 Industries: Oil, Trade, Constructions. We could Interview the CEOs and the CFOs of the Top Companies.
- private investors (as per FORBES lists of the Middle East Region)

- Institutional investors as insurance companies, pension funds, sovereign wealth funds, investment managers, banks (to finance the early stage and the growing stage of the project)

One consideration needs to be addressed for the **category of the Investment managers**: studies have included investment managers in institutional assets (for example, IMF (2011) and Inderst, Kaminker & Stewart (2012)). But, as per Nelson, Pierpont and the World Economic Forum (2011), the investment managers are often under pressure to demonstrate top investment performance over the short/medium term, therefore they invest only in liquid assets themselves, so they can sell these assets if and when their investors withdraw their money.

Thus, most investment managers, including those managing pension assets, have liquid, relatively short-term portfolios and they do not invest in project type assets that would be aligned with renewable energy. The important exceptions are some private equity and infrastructure funds that specifically target direct investments in projects and require long-term lock-in periods.

Based on the analysis and the information mentioned above, the **statistical sample within the reference market** will respond to the following parameters:

- FORBES's Top companies within the selected sectors.
- CEO and CFO of the above companies.
- FORBES's best Private investors
- Institutional investors
- Private clients.

Reference market within a single specific Industry

The same model can be replicate inside each single Industry: let's assume for example that a manufacturer of building material products would like to enter in a new selected market: the primary search has be conducted investigating the appetite index inside the industry interviewing the following leading Industry players:

- CEO and CFO of the leading construction company in the Region
- QA/QC managers and Cost engineers of the leading construction company and the leading contracting companies
- Project specification manager of the Top Architectural groups
- Owner association and Top Developer and Real Estate companies

Findings of the Primary research

The survey will provide important results about the appetite of the prospect clients in the Selected Region and in terms of information provided by the Respondents that will highlight the conditions under which a potential Lead could become a real Client, or it could be feasible to enter in the selected market.

Additional findings that need to be analyzed are the following one:
- Primary search – statistical frequency
- Respondent business and professional profile
- Respondent, by Region, Area, in percent
- Respondent by yearly income
- Average of the total available capital per Respondent
- Timing of available capital, per Respondent or market segment, in percentage
- Respondent perception of the proposed product
- Challenges potentially faced by the Respondent, in order to be able to address their needs, as logistic easy access to the product, distribution channels, payment options, friendly user tools

KEY NOTE

Investigate the challenges potentially faced by the Respondent, in order to be able to address their needs

Note of caution to be added in the feasibility plan

This is **mandatory note** to be added to your feasibility study.

Let's assume that, despite all the efforts, the percentage of the Respondent is low. Even a number of 20% of Respondent is a significant representative of the statistical sample, but the limitations are clear as 80% of the sample didn't complete the survey.

The Respondents are among the most important players of your Region, thus their answers are valuable but are not exhaustive.

The data is statistically correct because it is properly justified in terms of Reference market and Statistical sample choice, the frequency of answer is a good % and their comment has given important 1278indication to answer to the business question of your Plan.

It is important to identify that this might not be an adequate representation of the Selected Region and others might have different opinion compared to the few responders.

THE APPETITE INDEX

We are now about to enter in one of the most important points of the strategic plan and our feasibility plan: **the creation of the Appetite Index** of your potential clients and financial investors

The analysis of the results of the primary search will provide the respondent's personal interest in buying or investing in your product, company or brand within the Selected Region.

INDUSTRY DEFINITION

Which is your Industry, Who is the customer, Value preposition, levels of Strategy

SECONDARY SEARCH

Industry review, supply and demand, Porter 5 Forces, PEST, SWOT, Firm Value Chain, timing market entry, Resources and capabilities, Economic indicators

PRIMARY RESEARCH

Statistical method of research, questionnaire creation

APPETITE INDEX OF CLIENTS AND INVESTORS

Investment conditions and buying conditions.

CONCLUSIONS

Viable Strategy definition, Business models definition

The main figures to be reported to the investors, stakeholders and to you are the following one:

- how many Respondent to the survey have provided complete details regarding the conditions under which they would buy or invest?
  Find the % towards the sample universe, and the % out of the total Respondents.
- Among these Respondents who is included? Are valuable Industry players? How much each one of them is impacting in % on the GDP creation of the selected Region? Which is their influence?
- Appetite Index: how many positive answers out of the total has been provided, for each category analyzed?
- To which Industry belong the majority of the respondents with higher appetite index, in %?
- How are they divided by Revenues? Company size in terms of annual revenues, salary, demographic region, of the respondent?

Investment criteria
Business models to attract Investors and buyers

The following part of the book describe the conditions to be asked and therefore required by potential financial investors that you might contact in order to gain new capital and investment for growth.

Having found the appetite index of your selected prospect Clients or Investor, bearing in mind also the note of caution previously mentioned, the survey has provided an additional series of information not available from the literature, and therefore unique for your strategic plan, as the conditions under which the respondents would be interested in investing the Selected Region.

Example of conditions in the investment industry are:
- Appetite Index divided by Industry
- IRR required
- way to take part to the investment (equity, debts, buying distressed companies)
- target time frame for return of the capital
- Risk mitigation
- target range of leverage
- Exit strategy required (IPO, secondary market, Equity)

Looking further into the results, the findings of the primary research stage have provided the **best combination of factors** to be taken in consideration to achieve the highest response from all the potential customer or investors related by your strategic plan.

DEFINITIONS

If you are about to investigate the appetite index of potential investors it is important to recap the definition of the main terms that will be presented:

IRR

The Internal Rate of Return (IRR) is the discount rate that makes the net present value (NPV) of a project zero. In other words, it is the expected compound annual rate of return that will be earned on a project or investment.

If the IRR is greater than or equal to the cost of capital, the company would accept the project as a good investment.

If the IRR is lower, then it would be rejected.

IRR Calculation

Below is described an example of how to calculate the Internal Rate of Return IRR

A company is deciding whether to purchase a new machine that costs for instance $500,000. The life of the new asset is estimated to be four years and it is expected to generate an additional $160,000 of annual profits. In the fifth year, the company plans to sell the equipment for its salvage value of $50,000.

Meanwhile, another similar investment option can generate a 10% return. This is higher than the company's current hurdle rate of 8%. The goal is to make sure the company is making better use of its cash.

From a financial point of view, the company should make the purchase because the IRR is both greater than the hurdle rate and the IRR for the alternative investment.

Year	Cash Flows	PV of Cash Flows
0	-$500,000	-$500,000
1	$160,000	$141,247
2	$160,000	$124,692
3	$160,000	$110,077
4	$160,000	$97,176
5	$50,000	$26,808

NPV	0	
IRR	13%	

Excel was used to calculate the IRR, using the function =IRR().

Risk Mitigation
The process by which an organization introduces specific measures to minimize unacceptable risks associated with its operations.
Risk mitigation measures can be directed towards reducing the severity of risk consequences, reducing the probability of the risk materializing, or reducing the organizations exposure to the risk.

Exit strategy
The way in which an investor plans to close out an investment. For example, a venture capitalist or angel investor may look to an IPO or acquisition as his/her exit strategy.

Leverage
The degree to which a business is utilizing borrowed money.

Companies that are highly leveraged may be at risk of bankruptcy if they are unable to make payments on their debt; they may also be unable to find new lenders in the future.
The leverage is not always bad, however it can increase the shareholder's return on investment and often there are tax advantages associated with borrowing.

Primary research – example of questions

In order to obtain a source of valuable information and be able to **generate a numeric appetite index**, the type of questions has to be properly selected.

A quick overview of the type of question that can be used is the following one:

- Closed-questions: yes/no
- Like- type scale.
  Example: Using a scale of 1 to 5 where 1 means strongly agree and 5 means strongly disagree, how much do you agree or disagree with the following statements.
- Multiple choice questions: to ask the respondent to choose between two or more answer options. Questions can be as simple as "yes/no" or can give a choice of multiple answers
- Forced preferences rank order. The respondent must complete a sequential ranking from high to low until all factors are ranked
- Open/end, final, questions: the respondents are required to provide their own opinion. It can be used to understand better **their needs**

Example of questions to be addressed to potential investors

Source: MBA mastery project of Eng. Fabrizio Nicoli, CASS Business school, City University London

PART 1 – Company / Investor / Client Information

- Company Name/ Investor Name / Client name.
- Job position
- Industry

  Transportation & Heavy Equipment

  Financial Services (please specify _____)

  Energy - oil & gas – renewable - Utilities

  Electronics & Telecom

  Chemicals & Plastics

  Information Services

  Real Estate & Construction

  Pharmaceuticals & Biotechnology

  Retail & Retail Distribution / Consumer Products

  Food & Beverage

  hospitality

  Metal - mining, smelter, fabrication

  Other (please specify _____)
- Country of residence (for private investor)
- Company size (employees) and (sales)

Funding sources -fund
- General description of finance source
- Total available capital of source/fund
- Timing of available capital source
- Type of financial vehicle (Debt or Equity)

PART 2 – INVESTMENT OVERVIEW

In this section, we would like to know your view on the overall Investment activity on a specific project or product

Over the next 12 months, do you expect the **Investment activity** from the investors to:

Increase significantly

Increase slightly

Stay the same

Decrease slightly

Decrease significantly

In your view, what will be the drivers behind this trend?

Resilience compared to other markets

Macro-economic conditions

Political climate

Internal investor demand

External investor demand target available

Target price

Consolidation opportunities

Regulatory issues

Tax issues

Other (please specify)

In which sectors do you expect the highest **Investment activity (next 12 months?)**

SECTOR A
- o   Product or project A
- o   Product or project B

SECTOR B
- o   Product or project C
- o   Product or project D
- o   Other

What do you see as the biggest challenges for regional stakeholders to invest in the project or buy the product?

PART 3 – INVESTMENT CRITERIA

In this section we would like to know <u>your interest in investing</u> in the project or buying the product

- Preferred project: highlight in which project/product you might be interested in

Sector A
    Product or project A
    Product or project B
    Other (please specify _____)

Sector B
    Product or project C
    Product or project D
    Other (please specify_____)

- Typical investment size
- Target range of leverage
- Target time frame for return of capital
- Target ROI
- Target IRR
- Necessary or preferred risk mitigation (collateral, PPA, gov't guarantee, etc)
- Preferred Exit strategy (secondary market, sale to strategic, etc)
- Preferred Investment/capital structure
- Due diligence process
- Geographic target/limits

- Currency target/limits
- Political target/limits
- Would you prefer to take part to the investment with Equities (shares) or buying Debt

In the next year, your investment plan is likely to

Increase

remain unchanged

decrease

Primary research Survey – Example of questions to be addressed to a potential customer for pricing study

About how many units of this new product would you buy over the next year at each price point listed below?
FMV + 30% - FMV + 20% - FMV + 10% - FMV + 5% - - FMV - 5% - FMV - 10% - FMV - 20% - FMV - 30%

How would you best describe your familiarity with a product/service like that ?
I was not aware of such a product/service - Only generally aware - Have investigated or researched such products - Have been demoed with a product like this - Have purchased or regularly use a product like this

If you are a current user, how long have you used [Product/Service]?
Under 1 month - 1-6 months - 6 months to 1 year - 1-2 years - 3 years or more - not currently use

How often could you find a use for this [Product/Service]?
Once a week or more often - 2-3 times a month - Once a month - Every 2-3 months - 2-3 times a year - Once a year - Do not use

Based on the description, how interested would you be in buying this new [Product/Service] if priced within your budget?
Not at all interested - Not very interested - Not sure - Somewhat interested - Very interested

Which of the following best describes your need for this product?
I really need this product because nothing else can solve this problem - This is a minor improvement over what I currently use. - Looks okay but is about the same as what I'm using now. - My current product would serve me better. - I am not at all interested

At what price would this new product begin to look inexpensive or cheap? Select one.
FMV + 30% - (same as above) - FMV - 30%

At what price would the product begin to look too expensive? Select one. FMV + 30% - (same as above) - FMV - 30%

At what price would the product begin to look so expensive that you would never consider buying it?
FMV + 30% - (same as above) - FMV - 30%

Source: questionpro.com/survey-templates/concept-evaluation-and-pricing-study/

Appetite Index- Graphic example

Following the quantitative and qualitative results obtained by the survey, it is now time to analyze the data in order to identify the information of your interest.

Below are shown few example of graphic representation of the appetite index divided by product and sectors.

Let's assume that in the sector B the potential clients or investor are mainly interested in the product or project A: The focus of your strategy will be to satisfy the need of the customers towards the product/project A, avoiding a waste of time and resources on the other projects.

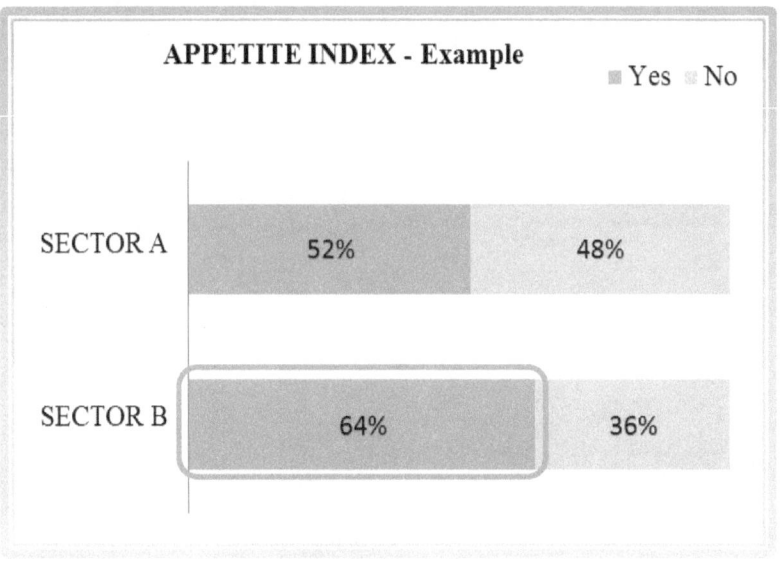

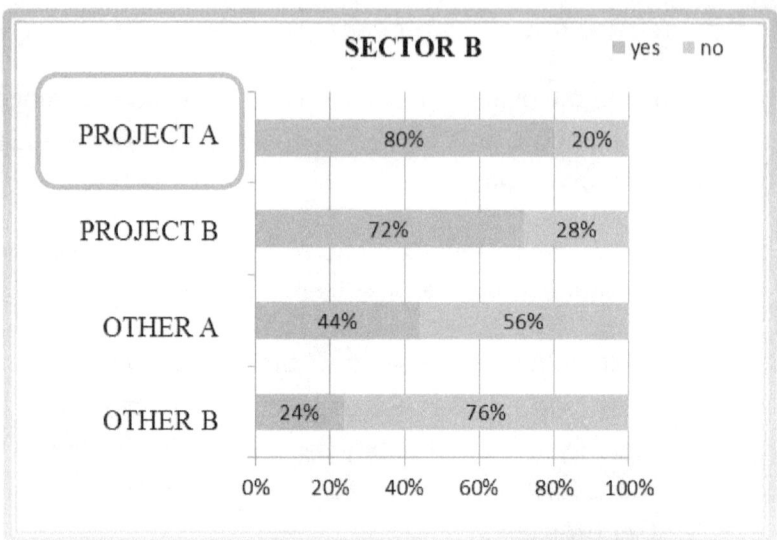

Another graphic representation of the results obtained from the primary search could tell us which product / project is preferred by each Industry player / private Investor / Institutional Investor, and so on.

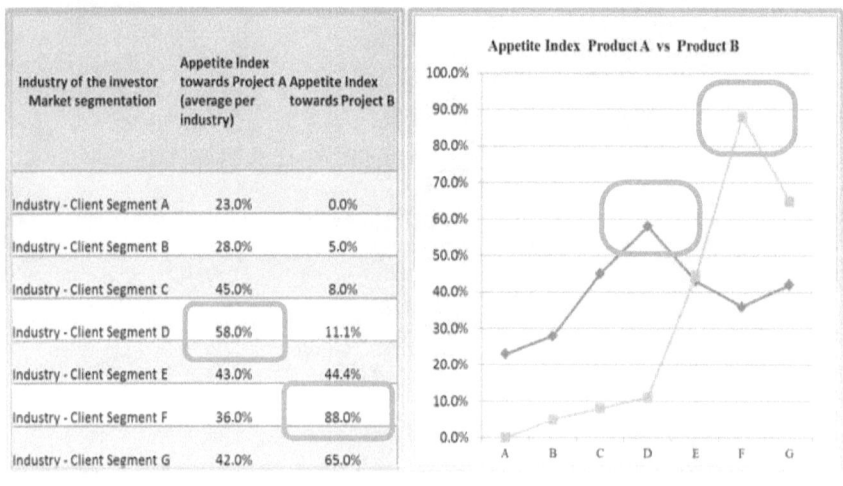

Additional results obtained by the primary research can highlight you also the **economic conditions under which financial investors could be interested in invest in your business.**

A graphic representation of it is shown in the below tables.
For instance, the companies of the Industry A might be interested in investing in your business if they will be granted a ROI of 20%, an IRR of the 30%, if they can participate to the investment with Equities and not debt, and if they can exit from the investment by an IPO. And so on.

Industry- Market segment A Appetite Index 65 %	
ROI Required	20%
IRR required	30 %
Way to take part to the Investment	Equity
Exit strategy required	IPO

Industry - Market segment B Appetite Index 48 %	
IRR required	21% (100 % of the Respondents)
Target time frame for return of capital	0-5 years (80xz% of the Respondents)
Way to take part to the Investment	Equities (60% of the Respondents)

Industry - Market segment C Appetite Index 73%	
IRR required	30% (60 % of Respondents)
Target range of leverage	70% debt/30% equity (70% of Respondents)
Risk mitigation	Limited recourse project finance (50% Respondent)

Industry - Market segment E Appetite Index 95 %	
Time frame for return of capital	Above 10 years (z % of Respondents)
Way to take part to the Investment	Equity (30 % of Respondents)
Risk mitigation	Government Guarantee (40 % Respondent)

Source: MBA mastery project of Eng. Fabrizio Nicoli, CASS
Business school, City University London.

CHAPTER
FIVE

CONCLUSIONS

&

VIABLE STRATEGY

TO EXPLOIT THE MARKET

CHAPTER 5

CONCLUSIONS

"Any intelligent fool can make things bigger and more complex. It takes a touch of genius – and a lot of courage – to move in the opposite direction"

Albert Einstein

The feasibility plan aim is to test whether private customers, private and institutional investors are willing to buy or invest in your product within the selected Region, in addition to defining the economic conditions under which they would be interested in doing it.

The study has been initially focused to cover the potential lack of information regarding the buyers, Clients and investors' appetite towards your product and the long term plan to expand your operation within the Selected Region.

After having defined your Industry, it has been carried out a review of the Industry and a review of the flow of investments both on a global than a local scale (secondary research).

The secondary research has provided the following important results and information:

- how has changed the supply and demand in the past years
- which are the main economic indicator to be analyzed in your Region
- how are the Countries policies impacting on your industry
- how is the projection of the supply-demand- investments and the trend in the Region
- which are the key competitive advantages of the competitors
- which could be the new entrants

The economic and political analysis show if the selected Region is currently experiencing political stability and GDP per capita growth, which is the main sector impacting in the creation of GDP and wealth of the Region; how is the demographic growth and how is connected to the demand of your product; governmental policies aim to support the companies and the investors to move in the selected Region in your field

Following the secondary search, a primary search has been carried out in order to define the Appetite Index of potential Clients and Investors towards your product.

The primary research is a survey provided to each of the local Industry decision makers that are having an important impact in the creation of the GDP of the selected Region or that are leading key players within your Industry.

The primary and secondary researches have highlighted key factors that need to be taken in consideration in order to create value and capture the value from the market, as:

- Product to be offered
- Appetite Index
- Business model to be used to enter in the selected Region based on the results of the primary research

It has been investigated about:

1. Value creation and Value capturing
2. Timing of market entry (leader, followers, not enter)
3. Resource and capability
4. Implement a Differentiation strategy or a Cost based strategy (Porter source of competitive advantage)
5. Value proposition creation
6. IMC Integrated Marketing Communication

   Eventually raise awareness of your brand through a new integrated marketing communication plan, focusing on advertising, personal selling, PR and events, direct marketing, sales promotions

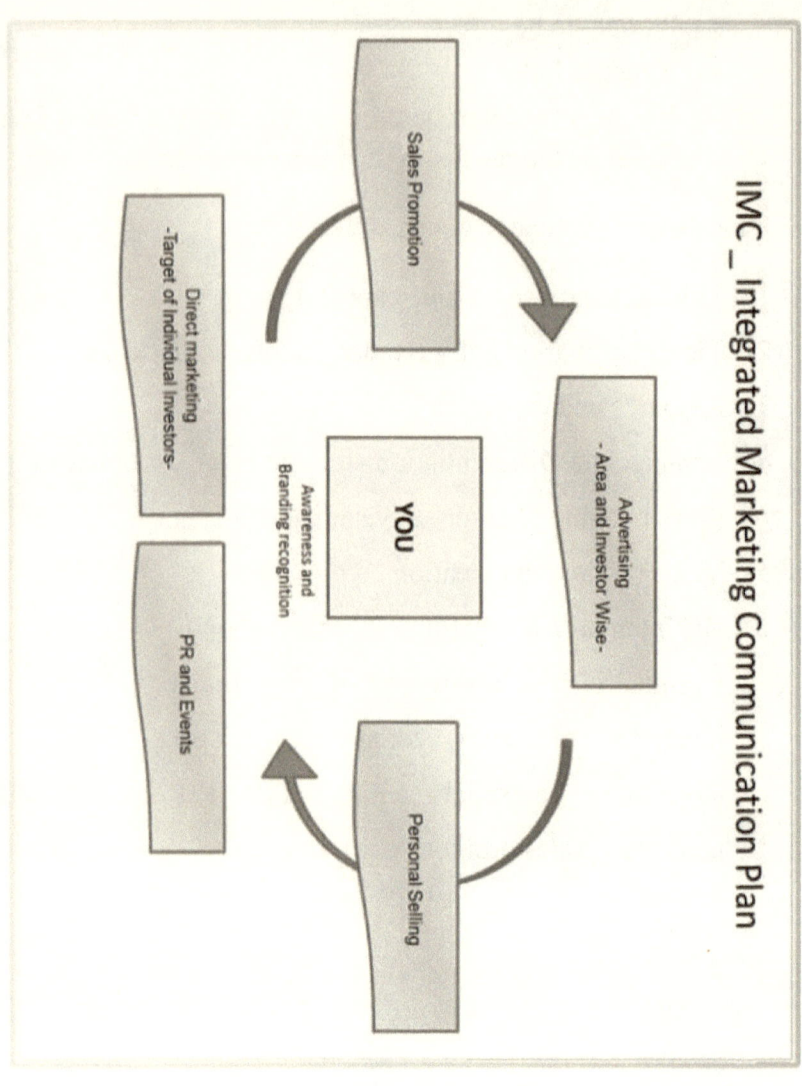

IMC _ Integrated Marketing Communication Plan

Sales Promotion

Advertising
- Area and Investor Wise-

Direct marketing
-Target of Individual Investors-

YOU

Awareness and
Branding recognition

PR and Events

Personal Selling

7. Improvement of the competitive output

- Superior concept of Technology, Pricing strategy based on the result of the primary search, Integrated marketing communication strategy;
- Increasing the switching costs towards the projects or investments of the competitors;
- Higher differentiation compared to the competitors

8. To target Countries that show a higher level of improvement in Governance in the long term, and a high level of deal activity in the short term (World Bank, 2004).
Better governance improves the investment climate by improving bureaucratic performances and predictability, which in turn reduces uncertainty, therefore governance and private investment are positively correlated (World Bank, 2006)

"As a matter of fact, it's pretty much all we talk about."

A good indicator of successful strategy?
A good indicator are profits… that will happen.
But …All we can see are profits… that have happened

GLOSSARY

Selected terms used in the strategy

Subject-specific glossaries can be found quite easily from the reading that you can do after the Successful Strategy for business growth. This is more personal.

Some of the entries have been used in this book while others are simply terms about learning that I believe should be known.

Absolute cost advantage cost advantage that is enjoyed by incumbents in an industry that new entrants cannot match.

Acquisition and restructuring strategy A strategy in which a company acquires inefficient and poorly managed enterprises and creates value by putting a superior financial governance structure in place in these acquired companies.

Acquisition A company's use of capital such as stock, debt, or cash to purchase another company.

Agency problem A problem that arises when managers pursue strategies that are not in the interests of stockholders.

Agency relationship A relationship that arises whenever one party delegates decision-making authority or control over resources to another.

Agent A person to whom authority is delegated by a principal.

Autonomous action Action taken by lower-level managers who on their own initiative formulate new strategies and work to persuade top-level managers to alter the strategic priorities of a company.

Bargaining power of buyers The ability of buyers to bargain down prices charged by companies in the industry or to raise the costs of companies in the industry by demanding better product quality and service.

Bargaining power of suppliers The ability of suppliers to raise the price of inputs or to raise the costs of the industry

Barriers to entry Factors that make it costly for companies to enter an industry.

Barriers to imitation Factors that make it difficult for a competitor to copy a company's distinctive competencies.

Behavior control A system of control based on the establishment of a comprehensive system of rules and procedures to direct the actions or behavior of divisions, functions, and individuals.

Brand loyalty Preference of consumers for the products of established companies.

Broad differentiator A company that offers a product designed for each market niche.

Business process Any business activity, such as order processing, inventory control, or product design, that is vital to delivering goods and services to customers quickly or that promotes high quality or low costs.

Business unit A self-contained division (with its own functions---for example, finance, purchasing, production, and marketing departments) that provides a product or for a particular   market.

Business-level strategy   The plan of action strategic managers adopt to use a company's resources and distinctive competencies to gain a competitive advantage.

Benchmarking   The comparison of similar processes across organizations and industries to measure progress, identify best practices, and set improvement targets. Results may serve as potential targets for key performance indicators.

Budget   description of the funding of existing or proposed actions.

Business Plan -These comprise the Corporate, Directorate, Service and Team plans, which specify the key priorities and activities to be undertaken.

Capabilities   A company's skills at coordinating its resources and putting them to productive use.

Capital productivity   Output per unit of invested capital.

Competitive advantage   A company is said to have a competitive advantage over its rivals when its profitability is greater than the average profitability for all firms in its industry.

Concentration on a single industry   The strategy a company adopts when it focuses its resources and capabilities on competing successfully within a particular product market.

Consolidated industry An industry dominated by a small number of large companies or, in extreme cases, by just one company, which are in a position to determine industry prices.

Corporate governance The mechanisms that exist to ensure that managers pursue strategies in the interests of an important stakeholder group, the shareholders.

Cost-leadership strategy A strategy of trying to outperform competitors by doing everything possible to produce goods or services at a cost lower than they do.

Customer defection rate The percentage of a company's customers who defect every year to competitors.

Customer needs Desires, wants, or cravings that can be satisfied by means of the characteristics of a product or service.

Customization Varying the features of a good or service to tailor it to the unique needs or tastes of groups of customers or, in the extreme case, of individual customers.

Cause and Effect The way perspectives, objectives, and/or measures interact in a series of cause-and-effect relationships demonstrate the impact of achieving an outcome. For example, organizations may hypothesize that the right employee training (Employee, Learning and Growth Perspective) will lead to increased innovation (Internal Process Perspective), which will in turn lead to greater customer satisfaction (Customer Perspective) and drive increased revenue (Financial Perspective).

Critical Success factor (CSF) A CSF is a business event, dependency, product that, if not attained, would seriously impair the likelihood of achieving a business objective.

Customer Perspective Measures are developed based on an organization's value proposition in serving their target customers.

Dashboard A dashboard is a reporting tool that consolidates, aggregates and arranges measurements, metrics (measurements compared to a goal) and sometimes scorecards on a single screen so information can be monitored at a glance. Dashboards differ from scorecards in being tailored to monitor a specific role or generate metrics reflecting a particular point of view

Declining industry industry with declining primary demand

Devil's advocacy A technique in which one member of a decision-making group acts as a devil's advocate, bringing out all the considerations that might make the proposal unacceptable.

Differentiation strategy A strategy of trying to achieve a competitive advantage by creating a product that is perceived by customers as unique in some important way.

Differentiation The way in which a company allocates people and resources to organizational tasks and divides them into functions and divisions so as to create value.

Distinctive competency A unique, firm-specific strength that enables a company to better *differentiate* its products and/or achieve substantially *lower costs* than its rivals and thus gain a competitive advantage.

Diversification Entering into one or more industries that are distinct or different from a company's core or original industry to find ways to use the company's distinctive competencies to increase the value to customers of the products it offers in those industries.

Diversified company A company that operates in two or more industries to find ways to increase long-run profitability.

Divestment strategy A strategy in which a company sells off its business assets and resources to other companies.

Divestment Selling a business unit to the highest bidder.

Economies of scale Reductions in unit costs attributed to a larger   output.
Efficiency The quantity of inputs that it takes to produce a given output (that is, efficiency = outputs/inputs).

Exit barriers The economic, strategic, and emotional factors that prevent companies from leaving an industry.

External stakeholders Individuals and groups outside the company that have some claim on the company.

Economic Value Added (EVA) A financial performance measure aiming to determine whether a company or activity has truly created shareholder value; in other words, EVA aims to distinguish real profit from paper profit. EVA is determined by calculating a business's after-tax cash flow minus the cost of the capital it deployed to generate that cash flow.

Focus strategy   A strategy of serving the needs of one or a few customer groups or segments.

Fragmented industry   An industry that consists of a large number of small or medium-sized companies, none of which is in a position to determine industry prices.

Franchising   A specialized form of licensing in which the franchiser sells the franchisee intangible property (normally a trademark) and insists that the franchisee agree to abide by strict rules about how it does business.

Financial Perspective – The perspective that looks at bottom line results. In public sector and non-profit organizations, the Financial Perspective is often viewed within the context of the constraints under which the organization must operate.

Forecast – Forecast usually refers to a projected value for a metric. Organizations will often create a forecast that is different than their target for a given metric.

Global standardization strategy   A strategy that focuses on increasing profitability by reaping the cost reductions derived from economies of scale and location economies.

Goal   A precise and measurable desired future state that a company attempts to realize.

Governance mechanisms   Mechanisms that principals put in place to align incentives between principals and agents and to monitor and control agents.

Growth industry   An industry where demand is expanding as first-time consumers enter the market.

Harvest strategy   The halting of investment in a business unit to maximize short-to-medium-term cash flow from that unit.

Horizontal differentiation   The process by which strategic managers choose how to divide people and tasks into functions and divisions to increase their ability to create value.

Horizontal integration   Acquiring or merging with industry competitors to achieve the competitive advantages that come with large size.

Human Capital – A metaphor for the transition in organizational value creation from physical assets to the capabilities of employees. Knowledge, skills, and relationships, for example.

Industry   A group of companies offering products or services that are close substitutes for each other---that is, products or services that satisfy the same basic customer needs.

Information asymmetry   A situation in which one party to an exchange has more information than the other party.

Innovation   The creation of new products or processes.

Intangible resources   Nonphysical entities that are the creation of managers and other employees, such as brand names, the reputation of the company, the knowledge that employees have gained through experience, and the intellectual property of the company, including that protected through patents, copyrights, and   trademarks.

Integration   The means a company uses to coordinate people, functions, and divisions to accomplish organizational tasks.

Internal new venture   A company's creation of the value chain functions necessary to start a new business from scratch.

Internal stakeholders   Stockholders and employees, including executive officers, other managers, and board members.

International licensing   An arrangement whereby a foreign licensee buys the rights to produce a company's product in the licensee's country for a negotiated fee.

International strategy   Companies pursuing an international strategy centralize product development functions such as R&D at home. They tend to establish manufacturing and marketing functions in each major country or geographic region in which they do business.

Joint venture   A formal type of strategic alliance in which two companies jointly create a new, separate company to enter a new product market or industry.

Key Performance Indicator (KPI) – Distinguished from other metrics, key performance indicators (KPIs) are those metrics most critical to gauging progress toward objectives. KPIs are metrics that are: tied to an objective; have at least one defined time-sensitive target value; and have explicit thresholds which grade the gap between the actual value and the target.

Leadership strategy   A strategy through which a company seeks to become the dominant player in a declining industry.

Lean production   A range of manufacturing technologies designed to reduce setup times for complex equipment, increase the use of individual machines through better scheduling, and improve quality control at all stages of the manufacturing process.

Learning effects   Cost savings that come from learning by doing.

Liquidation strategy   The shutting down of the operations of a business unit and the sale of its assets.

Localization strategy   A strategy that focuses on increasing profitability by customizing the company's goods or services so that they provide a good match to tastes and preferences in different national markets.

Macroenvironmental   The broader economic, global, technological, demographic, social, and political context in which an industry is embedded.

Management buyout (MBO)   The sale of a business unit to its current management

Market development   A strategy involving a search for new market segments, and therefore new uses, for a company's products.

Market penetration   A strategy in which a company concentrates on expanding market share in its existing product markets

Market segmentation   The way a company decides to group customers based on important differences in their needs or preferences, to gain a competitive advantage

Marketing strategy   The position that a company takes with regard to pricing, promotion, advertising, product design, and distribution.

Mass customization   The ability of companies to use flexible manufacturing technology to customize output at costs normally associated with mass production.

Mature industry   An industry where the market is saturated, demand is limited to replacement demand, and growth is slow.

Merger   An agreement between two companies to pool their operations and create a new business entity.

Measure (also called metric) – Term to describe a standard used to communicate progress on a particular aspect of a program. Measures typically are quantitative in nature, conveyed in numbers, dollars, percentages, etc. (e.g., $ of revenue, headcount number, % increase, survey rating average, etc.)

Metric (also called measure) – A framework to establish and collect measurements of success/failure on a regulated, timed basis that can be audited and verified.

Mission   What it is that the company exists to do.

Multidivisional company A company that competes in several different businesses and has created a separate, self-contained division to manage each of them.

Opportunistic exploitation Occurs when the managers of a firm seek to unilaterally rewrite the terms of a contract with suppliers, buyers, or complement providers in a way that is more favorable to the firm, often using their power to force the revision   through.

Organizational culture The specific collection of values and norms that are shared by people and groups in an organization and that control the way they interact with each other and with stakeholders outside the organization.

Organizational design The process through which managers select the combination of organizational structure and control systems that they believe will enable the company to create and sustain a competitive advantage.

Output control A system of control in which strategic managers estimate or forecast appropriate performance goals for each division, department, and employee and then measure actual performance relative to these goals.

Objective concise statement describing specific, actionable and measurable things an organization must do in order to effectively execute its strategy and achieve its mission and vision.

Operational Alignment The means to and/or state of alignment of an organization's day-to-day activities with its strategic goals or objectives, operational alignment helps ensure that an organization's daily activities are advancing its longer-term goals and mission.

Operational Performance Management A type of performance management that addresses the growing pressure to increase revenue while managing costs, while meeting ever-evolving and expanding customer demands.

Outcome Commonly used within the Logic Model, outcomes (also called outcome-impacts) describe the benefits that result as a consequence of an organization's investments and activities.

Output Commonly applied within the Logic Model, outputs describe what an organization gets done; e.g., "what we do" or "what we offer" and may include workshops, delivery of services, conferences, community surveys or facilitation.

Positioning strategy The specific set of options a company adopts for a product on four main dimensions of marketing: price, distribution, promotion and advertising, and product features.

Potential competitors Companies that are not currently competing in an industry but have the capability to do so.

Price leadership The process by which one company informally takes the responsibility for setting industry prices.

Price signaling The process by which companies increase or decrease product prices to convey their competitive intentions to other companies.

Primary activities Activities related to the design, creation, and delivery of the product, its marketing and after-sale service.

Principal A person delegating authority to an agent, who acts on the principal's behalf.

Process innovation The development of a new process for producing products and delivering them to customers.

Product bundling The strategy of offering customers the opportunity to buy a complete range of products at a single, combined price.

Product development A strategy involving the constant creation of new or improved products to replace existing ones

Product differentiation The process of creating a competitive advantage by designing goods to satisfy customer needs. **Product innovation** The development of products that are new to the world or have attributes superior to those of existing products.

Profitability The return that a company makes on the capital invested in the enterprise.

Performance Driver – Measures that indicate progress against a process or behaviour. These measures are helpful in predicting the future outcome of an objective.

Qualitative – Subjective, as opposed to quantitative (measured). A common source of qualitative metrics are surveys of customers, stakeholders or employees.

Quantitative – Measured, as opposed to qualitative (subjective). Quantitative measures often come from transactional systems.

Reengineering A process whereby, in their effort to boost company performance, managers focus not on the company's functional activities but on the business processes underlying its value creation operations.

Related diversification The strategy of operating a business unit in a new industry that is related to a company's existing business units through some commonality in their value chains.

Resources Financial, physical, social or human, technological, and organizational factors that allow a company to create value for its customers. Company resources can be divided into two types: tangible and intangible resources.

Risk capital Equity capital for which there is no guarantee that stockholders will ever recoup their investment or earn a decent return.

Rivalry The competitive struggle between companies in an industry to gain market share from each other.

Spinoff The sale of a business unit to another company or to independent investors.

Stakeholders Individuals or groups with an interest, claim, or stake in the company, in what it does, and in how well it performs.

Standardization The degree to which a company specifies

how decisions are to be made so that employees' behavior becomes predictable.

Strategy is the way an organization seeks to achieve its vision and mission. It is a forward-looking statement about an organization's planned use of resources and deployment capabilities. Strategy becomes real when it is associated with: set of goals and objectives; and a method involving people, resources, processes.

Strategic alliance A cooperative agreement between two or more companies to work together and share resources to achieve a common business objective.

Strategic change The movement of a company away from its present state toward some desired future state to increase its competitive advantage and profitability.

Strategic control systems target-setting, measurement, and feedback systems that enable strategic managers to evaluate whether a company is implementing its strategy successfully.

Strategy formulation Analyzing the organization's external and internal environments and then selecting appropriate strategies.

Strategy execution: Putting strategies into action.

Strategic Management System Describes the use of the Balanced Scorecard in aligning an organization's short-term actions with strategy.

Strategy Map A specific version of a strategy plan that adheres to the Balanced Scorecard methodology. Strategy maps depict objectives in multiple perspectives with corresponding cause and effect linkages.

Strategy Plan A visual representation of an organization's strategy and the objectives that must be met to effectively reach its mission. A strategy plan can be used to communicate, motivate and align the organization to ensure successful execution.

Strategic responsibility In the multidivisional structure, responsibility of managers at corporate headquarters for overseeing long-term plans and providing guidance for divisional managers.

Substitute products The products of different businesses or industries that can satisfy similar customer needs.

Support activities: Activities of the value chain that provide inputs that allow the primary activities to take place.

Sustained competitive advantage A company has a sustained competitive advantage when it is able to maintain above-average profitability for a number of years.

Switching costs Costs that consumers must bear to switch from the products offered by one established company to the products offered by a new entrant.

SWOT analysis The comparison of strengths, weaknesses, opportunities, and threats.

Scorecard visual display of the most important information needed to achieve one or more objectives, consolidated and arranged on a single screen so the information can be monitored at a glance. Unlike dashboards that display actual values of metrics, scorecards typically display the gap between actual and target values for a smaller number of key performance indicators.

Six Sigma A quality management and process improvement methodology suited to process intensive industries like manufacturing. Six Sigma measures a given process by its average performance and the standard deviation of this performance, aiming to reduce the occurrence of defects to a level of "Six Sigma" outside the norm; no more than 3.4 times per million.

Target – A target is the defining standard of success, to be achieved over a specified time period, for the key performance indicators associated with a particular strategic objective.

Value Chain – The process steps by which a company moves from the identification of its customer needs to customer fulfilment.

Value Proposition – Describes how an organization intends to differentiate itself in the marketplace and what particular value it will deliver to customers. Many organizations choose one of three "value disciplines" operational excellence, product leadership, or customer intimacy.

Vertical differentiation   The process by which strategic managers choose how to distribute decision-making authority over value creation activities in an organization.

Vertical integration   A strategy in which a company expands its operations either backward into industries that produce inputs for its core products (*backward vertical integration*) or forward into industries that use, distribute, or sell its products (*forward vertical   integration*).

Virtual corporation   A company that outsources most of its functional activities and focuses on one or a few core value chain functions

Vision   A concise statement defining an organization's long-term direction, the vision is a summary statement of what the organization ultimately intends to become five, 10 or even 15 years into the future. It is the organization's long-term "dream," what it constantly strives to achieve.

BIBLIOGRAPHY

- Annual Economic Report 2012, United Arab Emirates, Ministry of Economy
- Baldacci, Clements, Gupta, Cui (2004), 'Social Spending, Human Capital, and Growth in Developing Countries:Implications for Achieving the MDGs' , IMF Working Paper WP/04/217, 2004
- Blakes lawyers, Gulf Cooperation Council Investment Outlook
- Bloomberg new energy finance BNEF' North-South clean energy investment reaches just $8bn per annum' [Online] Available from: http://about.bnef.com/press-releases/north-south-clean-energy-investment-reaches-just-8bn-per-annum-2/
- Bloomberg new energy finance BNEF, 'Financial regulation – biased against clean energy and green infrastructure?' [Online] Available from: http://about.bnef.com/white-papers/financial-regulation-biased-against-clean-energy-and-green-infrastructure
- BreakThrough visual Cartoon [Online] Available from: www.breakthroughvisuals.com
- Bossdorf, Engels, Weiler (2013), 'EU GCC INVEST REPORT 2013, Promotion of Mutual investment opportunities and creation of a virtual European structure in the GCC', 2013
- BP Statistical review of World energy 2012
- CIF Corporate Finance Institute [Online] Available from: https://corporatefinanceinstitute.com
- CERES Org: 2012-investor-action-plan, [Online] Available from: https://www.ceres.org/incr-2/investor-summit/summit-files/2012-investor-action-plan
- Europe's environment An Assessment of Assessments 5 Recommendations, EEA
- Forbes global list 2000, The world biggest Public Companies [Online] available from: http://www.forbes.com/global2000/list/
- Forbes Middle East: Top 100 Family Business Making an impact in the arab world [Online] Available from: http://english.forbesmiddleeast.com/view.php?list=44476
- Forbes Middle East: Top 500 Companies in the Arab World and Top 100 Making an Impact [Online] Available from: http://english.forbesmiddleeast.com/view.php?list=44477

- Forbes: The world billionaires, [Online] Available from: http://www.forbes.com/billionaires/list/#page:1_sort:0_direction:asc _search:_filter:All%20industries_filter:United%20Arab%20Emirates _filter:All%20states
- GCC Economic Insight, 2012, QNB Qatar National Bank
- GCC trade and investment flows, The emerging-market surge, A report from the Economist Intelligence Unit Sponsored by Falcon & Associates, The Economist Intelligence Unit Limited 2011
- Gee, D. (2001), 'Business and the environment:current trends and developments in corporate reporting and ranking, Technical report No 54', European Environment Agency, 2001
- IMF Country Report No. 12/116, 2012 ARTICLE IV CONSULTATION
- IMF Survey: Mideast Oil Importers Under Strain, Oil Exporters Faring Well[Online] Available from: imf.org/external/pubs/ft/survey/so/2012/car042012d.htm
- IMF World Economic Outlook (WEO) Update -- Gradual Upturn in Global Growth During 2013, January 2013[Online] Available from: www.imf.org/external/pubs/ft/weo/2013/update/01/index.htm
- IMF: Regional Economic Outlook: Middle East and Central Asia, November 2012 [Online] Available from: www.imf.org/external/pubs/ft/reo/2012/mcd/eng/mreo1112.htm
- International Energy Agency (IEA) World Energy Outlook (2012)
- Investopedia: economic indicators to know by roger Wohlner [Online] Available from: www.investopedia.com/terms/i/indicator.asp www.investopedia.com/university/releases/
- Investorwords, terminologies and definitions [Online] Available from: www.investorwords.com/19332/risk_mitigation.html
- Mako, W. Sourrouille, D. (2010) ' Investment funds in MENA, financial flagship', The World Bank
- Ministry of Foreign affairs, United Arab Emirates, [Online] Available from: http://www.mofa.gov.ae/mofa_english/portal/2666c727-3cea-4483-9791-56462f752166.aspx
- National Bureau of Statistic, United Arab Emirates, [Online] Available from: www.uaestatistics.gov.ae/EnglishHome/tabid/96/Default.aspx

- Nicoli Fabrizio, executive MBA mastery project. CASS business School London. 2013.
- Nieto, J. (2008) 'A study of Private Investment in the Middle East and North Africa' ,Business Mastery Project, Cass Business School
- oecd-ilibrary.org [Online] Available from: www.oecd-ilibrary.org/economics/oecd-factbook-2015-2016_factbook-2015-en
- Outlook for the Gulf and the Global Economy the GCC in 2020, report from the Economist Intelligence Unit Sponsored by the Qatar Financial Centre Authority, The Economist Intelligence Unit Limited
- Porter: Competitive Advantage: Creating and Sustaining Superior Performance. 1985
- PEST analysis definition [Online] Available from: http://www.businessdictionary.com/definition/PEST-analysis.html#ixzz2ZcUTvfI0)
- Porter's five forces definition [Online] Available from: http://www.investopedia.com/terms/p/porter.asp
- Porter 5 Forces, Threat of new entrants [Online] Available from: www.cleverism.com/threat-of-new-entrants-porters-five-forces-model/ www.strategiccfo.com/threat-of-new-entrants-one-of-porters-five-forces/
- Prof. Alizadeh, A. Oil and Energy Trading, Transport & Risk Management, World Energy Markets and Trade, Unit 1, EMBA Dubai, CASS Business School, April 2013
- Prof. Halliburton, C. IMC Integrated Marketing Communication, EMBA Marketing Dubai, CASS Business School, December 2011
- Prof. Lanzolla, G. Strategy Course, EMBA Dubai, CASS Business School London, March 2012
- Prof.Jafree, K., ICFMV Equity Analysis framework, Applied Corporate Finance II, EMBA Dubai, CASS Business School, March 2013
- Question Pro, how to do market research [Online] Available from: https://opentoexport.com/article/how-to-do-market-research/ https://www.questionpro.com/blog/primary-research/
- Regional Economic Outlook, Middle East and Central Asia-Washington, D.C., IMF International Monetary Fund, 2012
- Reichelt, H. (2010) 'Green bonds: a model to mobilise private capital to fund climate change mitigation and adaptation projects' the

Euromoney environmetal finance handbook, The World Bank, 2010
- United Arab Emirates Economy Profile 2013, Index Mundi, [Online] Available from: www.indexmundi.com/united_arab_emirates/economy_profile.html
- United Arab Emirates: Economic Indicators,Data extracted from IMF Data warehouse on: 3/25/2013 2:55:40 PM, International Financial Statistics (IFS)
- World Bank Finances [Online] Available from: https://finances.worldbank.org/browse?browse_in_container=false&custom_class=catalog-home&sortBy=relevance&tags=beneficiaries&q=middle%20east%20flow%20investment
- World Bank Org: Bonds & Investment Products[Online] Available from: treasury.worldbank.org/cmd/htm/index.html
- World Bank org: Foreign direct investment, net inflows (BoP, current US$)[Online] Available from: http://data.worldbank.org/indicator/BX.KLT.DINV.CD.WD
- World Bank Org: World Development Indicators: six changes for 2013 [Online] Available from: http://blogs.worldbank.org/opendata/world-development-indicators-six-changes-for-2013
- Wikipedia: automotive Industry [Online] Available from: https://en.m.wikipedia.org/wiki/Automotive_industry

DISCLAIMER

Author: Engr. Fabrizio Nicoli, Italy, EMBA CASS Business School London. Email: fabrinicoli@gmail.com

This manual is designed to provide information in regard to the subject matter covered. It is sold with the understanding that the publisher and authors and advisers are not rendering legal, accounting or other professional services.

It is not the purpose of this manual to reprint all the information that is otherwise available to authors, printers and publisher but to complement, amplify and supplement other texts. For more information, see the references throughout the text. Every effort has been made to make this manual as complete and as accurate as possible. However, there may be mistakes both typographical and in content. Therefore, this text should be used only as a general guide and not as the ultimate source of publishing information. Furthermore, this manual contains information only up to the printing date.

The authors, advisers and publisher shall have neither liability nor responsibility to any person or entity with respect to any loss or damage caused or alleged to be caused directly or indirectly by the information contained in this manual.

Posizione nella classifica Bestseller di Amazon:

n.1 in Impresa, strategia e gestione (Libri in altre lingue)

n.1 in Inglese

n.1 in Impresa, strategia e gestione (Kindle Store)

Maggiori informazioni sull'autore

› Visita la pagina di FABRIZIO NICOLI su Amazon

Scopri i libri, conosci gli autori, leggi i blog degli autori e molto altro

✓ Segui

● https://www.amazon.br/dp/B07QQDS3LD

Détails sur le produit

Format : Format Kindle

Taille du fichier : 4904 KB

Utilisation simultanée de l'appareil : Illimité

Vendu par : Amazon Media EU S. à r.l.

Langue : Anglais

ASIN: B07QQDS3LD

Synthèse vocale : Non activée

X-Ray : Non activée

Word Wise: Non activé

Composition améliorée: Non activé

Moyenne des commentaires client : Soyez la première personne à écrire un commentaire sur cet article

Classement des meilleures ventes d'Amazon:

n°1 dans Systems & Planning (Livres anglais et étrangers)

n°1 dans Entrepreneurship (Livres anglais et étrangers)

n°1 dans Systems & Planning (Boutique Kindle)

Voulez-vous nous parler de prix plus bas?

En savoir plus sur l'auteur

› Consultez la page FABRIZIO NICOLI d'Amazon

Découvrez des livres, informez-vous sur les écrivains, lisez des blogs d'auteurs et bien plus encore

CITY
UNIVERSITY OF LONDON
—— EST 1894 ——

CASS
BUSINESS SCHOOL
CITY, UNIVERSITY OF LONDON

—— EST 1894 ——

R20
REGIONS OF
CLIMATE ACTION

MBA Thesis given the 'sign' of approval by Governor Arnold Schwarzenegger

Posted on by Danielle Critchley

Alumni Stories

Fabrizio Nicoli (Executive MBA in Dubai, 2014), shares how his fantastic opportunity to complete his MBA Thesis project at Governor Arnold Schwarzenegger's not-for-profit organisation, R20 – Regions of Climate Change, has secured him a representative role in the Middle East

...nd out more about Fabrizio ...ere

...an you tell me about your ...me at Cass?

...aving lived in Dubai for the last ...0 years, I undertook the ...xecutive MBA at the age of 31 ...t the institution in the United

**CONTACTS &
NEW BOOKS RELEASE**

Amazon.com Fabrizio Nicoli

www.fabrizionicoli.wixsite.com/ebook

FabrizioNicoliBook

linkedin.com/in/fabrizio-nicoli-mba/

www.ingramcontent.com/pod-product-compliance
Lightning Source LLC
Chambersburg PA
CBHW021407210526
45463CB00001B/253